Village Green

Village Green

Sermons from Asbury First United Methodist Church

ROBERT ALLAN HILL

RESOURCE *Publications* · Eugene, Oregon

VILLAGE GREEN
Sermons from Asbury First United Methodist Church

Copyright © 2011 Robert Allan Hill. All rights reserved. Except for brief quotations in critical publications or reviews, no part of this book may be reproduced in any manner without prior written permission from the publisher. Write: Permissions, Wipf and Stock Publishers, 199 W. 8th Ave., Suite 3, Eugene, OR 97401.

Resource Publications
An Imprint of Wipf and Stock Publishers
199 W. 8th Ave., Suite 3
Eugene, OR 97401

www.wipfandstock.com

ISBN 13: 978-1-61097-228-4

Manufactured in the U.S.A.

*To the congregation of Asbury First United Methodist Church,
Rochester, NY, with love and respect*

Contents

PART 1: Village Green

1. "Do You Hear the Promise?" / 3
2. "Can We Live with Promise?" / 11
3. "Can Promise Emerge from a Land of Plenty" / 18
4. "A Grain of Truth" / 25
5. "A Promise of Freedom and Love" / 32
6. "Don't Get Too Comfortable!" / 37
7. "A Promise Before Dark" / 45
   Homiletical Appendix / 52

PART 2: Once More to the Lake

8. Health / 56
9. Height / 63
10. Home / 69
11. Hope / 77
12. Heart / 83
13. Habit / 89
14. Hand / 97

PART 3: Empire Spirit

15. New York: The View from Ellis Island / 107
16. Albany: Crossing the Hudson / 116
17. Utica: The Far Side of Fear / 123
18. Ithaca: After the Fall / 131

19. Lake Placid: A Survey of Freedom / 135
20. Syracuse: A Wind at Midnight / 144
21. Elmira: The Saving Power of an Intervening Word / 152
22. Auburn: A Grateful Heart / 156
23. Buffalo: By Your Leave / 163
24. Rochester: Colorama / 169

Part 1

Village Green

1

"Do You Hear the Promise?"

Amos 4:1–2, 6:4–6; 2 Corinthians 1:15–22

1. SPIRE AND PULPIT

Baptist Church

THE BELLS ARE TOLLING this morning, singing out from the spire of a little church on a little street in a little town. In the town in which we were raised, during the bucolic years of the New Frontier, the beat and cadence of life were set by the Baptist church bells. Hourly they rang, and on Sunday they pealed out the call to faith like a rural minaret, a country shofar, the invitation to the living to hear something of the meaning of life. I noticed that they are repairing the roof and steeple again this year. For a church born in 1793, you expect some repairs. Colgate graduates like Harry Emerson Fosdick and Adam Clayton Powell worshipped in the worn pews, sitting before a simple and stern old regular Baptist pulpit. Like Rochester, Hamilton is a Baptist town, its deep structures still fixed according to the original, pilgrim design, and beginning with a place for a word fitly spoken.

Love of Words

This is a little town that is steadily filled with a kind of twilight breeze. The Baptist church bells there ring every hour, sonorous and stately. It is a quiet place, forgotten except for its college. Most of the farms around it have grown up to brush again. There is not a lot of activity in the park, or on the main street. But it is a place where words matter. Growing up, our mailman was a Colgate graduate. So was the barber. Some of the farmers who lead and funded the church were, too. There is a gentle hum of words fitly spoken up and down the little lanes of Hamilton, and the day ends at twilight with a sense of rest and deep gratitude, especially for what has been heard and for what has been said. In that village twilight, the magic of language so enthralls its citizens that they are its permanent captives, listening for a word of promise, trusting in a word of promise, walking toward the promise star, Polaris.

Still Small Voice

For all our vaunted material and visible power, the march of armies, the conquest of lands, the construction of cities, the stewardship of industry, the care of crops, the oversight of houses of worship, there is a still small voice, whispering at the edge of time and space, and speaking silently from the stars above, whose mute promise silences all else. How powerful is a word of promise! The prophets regretted promises broken. The apostles acclaimed a promise kept. Our souls stand or fall by words of promise. Today, this week, listen for promise!

2. A FAMINE OF THE WORD

Promises Unkept

Our Holy Scripture, truer to life than is our own experience, enshrines divine promise. Our promises fail sometimes, or fail in part much of the time. It is the mighty theme of the God who keeps God's promises that is carried in the pages of the Bible. The Prophets of old, like Hosea and Amos, who were hurt by broken human promises, held out a longing— no, a yearning—for the Kept Promise of God.

This is our condition: life amid fractured promises. Recently a church group planned over a fortnight in advance to gather for a serious, probing discussion of punctuality at the beginning and ending of meetings. The meeting began at 6:30 A. M. I woke up to see the clock at 6:40, and arrived at 7:00 A. M. In other words, I showed up late to a meeting about punctuality! That's like carrying a banana split into weight watchers, or going drunk to AA! But this is our condition, life amid punctured promises.

Amos Speaks

Eight hundred years before Jesus was born, the prophet Amos confronted Israel with broken promises. I have been in Rochester 5 years, and in these years, our nation has come more and more to resemble the Israel Amos rebuked. Amos asked his countryfolk to peek courageously underneath the comfortable quilt of prosperity, and see their impending doom. You have forgotten the poor. You are personally immoral. You trust too much in your military might. And your religion is a shallow as a mother in law's love. Said Amos. To Israel.

Amos prophesied that all manner of ill would befall the seemingly prosperous folks doing business in Jerusalem in the time of Jereoboam. He asserted that their prosperity was chimerical, and fleeting, and about to end. He forecasted all manner of doom for his people. The God of covenant keeps his promises, he preached. Beware.

To the women:

> *Hear this you cows of Bashan*
> *Who are in the mountains of Samaria*
> *Who oppress the poor*
> *Who crush the needy*
> *Who say to their husbands*
> *'Bring that we may drink'*
> *The Lord God has sworn by his holiness that*
> *Behold the days are coming upon you*
> *When they shall take you away with hooks*
> *Even the last of you with fish hooks.*

To the men:

> *Woe to you who are at ease in Zion*
> *The notable men of the first of the Nations*
> *Woe to those who lie upon beds of ivory*
> *And Stretch themselves upon their couches*
> *And eat lambs from the flock*
> *And calves from the midst of the stall*
> *Who sing idle songs to the sound of the harp*
> *And like David invent for themselves instruments of music*
> *Who drink wine in bowls*
> *And anoint themselves with the finest oil . . .*
> *But are not grieved over the ruin of Joseph!*[1]

---

1. Amos 4.

But at the end of his mighty litany of trouble—all of which eventually befell his people, though they prospered and ignored him in his lifetime—Amos predicts that a penultimate tragedy, unspeakable in its horror, will also befall Israel.

For Amos and for Israel and, though we laugh at it, for us, this is the worst of tragedies. Amos predicts a time when, for a time, there will be no promissory speech, no word of life. When the silence of God will be empty and void. Worse than slavery, worse than slaughter, worse than the bitterest of physical suffering - hear Amos's foreboding of life without promise:

> *Behold the days are coming says the Lord God*
> *When I will send a famine on the land*
> *Not a famine of bread, nor a thirst for water*
> *But of hearing the words of the Lord.*[2]

A life without a word of promise, words too of promise, is a life of dust and ashes, it is a living death.

10 years ago this summer, my closest cousin, Chuck was killed in a tragic work accident, leaving three preschool children and a traumatized widow. For a long time, then and after, all the words of prophecy and promise from faith and funeral and family went unheard, at least for me. His inexplicably random and tragically horrible death left a part of my heart cold and ear turned deaf. So it is with a famine of the word.

3. THE JOYFUL MESSAGE

Hearing Promise

To be healthy and happy, to be saved, to be set free, to hope for heaven, we need promises that are kept. 90% of this message is a simple reminder: God keeps God's promises. 10% is a not so simple reminder: we are most fully human when we try, though we are sure in part to fail, nonetheless to keep our own promises too.

How are we ever going to do this?

Not alone we are not.

But there is One in whom Promise lives.

---

2. Amos 8:11.

Pauline Promise

Our Holy Scripture, truer to life than is our own experience, enshrines divine promise. Our promises fail sometimes, or fail in part much of the time. It is the mighty theme of the God who keeps God's promises that is carried in the pages of the Bible. Then in the Joyful Testament, we are told of Jesus Christ. Do you remember how Paul put it? "For the Son of God, Jesus Christ, whom we preach among you, was not Yes and No; but in him it is always *Yes*. *"For all the promises of God find their Yes in him."*[3] We will listen again this fall to Paul. Jesus Christ is the Kept Promise of God. On him we cast our gaze, toward him we set our sights, by him we mark our progress, to him we walk by faith.

Jesus Christ is alive and busy in our world and your life. He may though have other interests than your current passions. See: he is nursing the weakest of newborn children. Look: he prays at the soup kitchen table of the poor. Watch: you will find him among the quiet giving people of the church. Listen: He speaks through the Holy Scripture and through the word rightly handled. But he does not coerce, he does not force, he does not rape. He speaks a word of promise.

Do you hear the promise?

Promise Lives

His voice still rings out, now and then, in prophetic utterance.

It is the memory of biblical prophecy that causes many in our time to rue the lack of truthfulness on the part of those entrusted with the highest and most powerful offices in the land. We feel the fear of the word famine. But the voice of truth, the spirit of Jesus Christ, will not be stilled! Sometimes you have to listen closely, but it is there!

Recall two years ago, this week, a prophetic voice, in the tradition of Amos, was heard: "I fear the President has undercut the efforts of millions of American parents who are naturally trying to instill in our children the value of honesty."[4] Over Labor Day, a Connecticut Senator and a Democrat had listened to his family, and alone went to the well of the Senate on September 3 1998 to make a powerful speech, recalling the prophetic utterance and the need for truth telling. I think I read somewhere that he is now a candidate for the Vice Presidency!

3. 2 Corinthians 1:20.
4. Senator Joe Liebermann, *New York Times*, September 4, 1998.

Remember also (to be bipartisan) this summer's Republican Convention when in a great moment of oratory, one leader decried our neglect of poor children, with a rhetorical gem, a golden phrase. "Woe" he said, "to those many who practice *the soft bigotry of low expectations*"[5] and in a flash a dozen of life came to mind, pleadings with the stone faced administrators of our city schools, appealing for a measure of safety of discipline of respect, and having - almost always in the eyes, and sometimes on the tongue - to hear this comment over the sea of mostly brown and mahogany and chestnut faces: "You know, Rev, these kids . . . you can't . . . I mean . . . they won't . . . you just can't expect them to behave and learn . . . Oh, Not Your Kids, Rev, but these . . ." The soft bigotry of low expectations. I only object to the word "soft." There is promise of truth told, by a political leader. I think I read somewhere that he is now a candidate for the Presidency!

4. A DAILY PROMISE

Your Promises

Our lives, when we are at our best, are filled to the brim with promise. We learn to depend on each other, and to trust another's promise. "Will you meet me after the game so we can talk?" Yes. "Can you pick me up after work?" Yes. "Can I tell you something in confidence, just between us?" Sure you can. "Will you marry me?" I will. "For better for worse, richer and poorer, sickness and health?" I do. "Promise me you will tell me when I make a fool of myself." I promise. "If I don't make it through surgery, will you watch out for my kids?" I will try. "What do think, really, is there love and life after death?" I believe it is so. "Promise me you will be faithful." I promise.

The Promise of a Better World

This summer in Prague, we saw the simple apartment where the Chech president lives. This is Vaclav Havel, 40 years a dissident, 30 years a playwright, 20 years an activist, 10 years in prison, now ill and dying, but through it all, a witness to the promise of a better world. In 1987, long before the wall came down, and after 40 years of failed struggle, he could write: "Hope is an ability to work for something because it is good, not

---

5. President George W. Bush.

just because it stands a chance to succeed." Havel, an agnostic, is part of the community of love and hope, a citizen of the North Star.

He reminds us that the Kingdom of God is not a state of mind, but a state of affairs, not spiritual but historical, and not here yet.

For ancient travelers like Hosea and Paul were guided at night by the North Star. There is a venerable tradition, many hundreds of years old, that connects Jesus Christ to the North Star. Our north star. He is the fixed point, the promise on which we base our lives. We live by trusting his promise. I think of Harriet Tubman and of Sojourner Truth and of Frederick Douglass and of countless slaves, running ahead of death toward freedom. They came north to freedom. They followed the North Star as they ran and walked and hid out and prayed. Some slept in houses and barns in our county, as they went north toward Canada.

This year, this fall, we will take another step or two, under the gleaming gaze of the North Star, in whom "it is always Yes."

5. THE NORTH STAR

Yes it was ten summers ago we were finishing a feast of corn and beef. That was a hot August 1990, and we had part of mind, at 9 pm to go for a swim under the clear later summer sky. We could see Ursa Major and Ursa Minor and the great North Star on the latter's tail. We saw Draco the Dragon and Queen Cassiopia in her chair. We saw the milky way, a filmy haze and dusting. The stars gleamed and beckoned. And then the phone rang bringing that hard news, that report, that my cousin Chuck had been killed in a work accident. He and a fellow phone company line man had been electrocuted. Because he was my closest cousin, because of his relative youth, because he left three toddler children, and because real loss means real grief, I bitterly prayed a doubting prayer that night, underneath the North Star.

Later that week the funeral came, and with it a sermon, brief and good that I dismissed in my anger. "Awful as this is, better days are coming", the preacher promised. "Weeping may tarry for the night, but joy comes with the morning", the Scripture promised. "In the seed a hidden promise, butterflies will soon be free", the choir promised. "We will get through this", the Word promised. I looked over at his widow and kids and cursed and doubted.

Jesus Christ is God's promise kept, by the ministry of the cross and through and struggling out through the real pain of life. Faith gives us power to withstand even when we do not understand, and to press on trusting in the promise: "A better day is coming. Hang on." A part of that day has come, at last. Today.

Today at 3 P. M. by God's grace, I will officiate at the wedding of Chuck's widow, taking vows of promise with a good man, not a replacement but a husband, and 3 teenagers will be bridesmaids and groomsmen. It took ten years, but a part of the promise has been kept. A measure of stability and happiness and joy has returned, a decade late(r).

When you gaze at the North Star tonight, remember the God who keeps God's promises.

As Unamuno wrote, *"Warmth Warmth Warmth! We are dying of cold, not of darkness! It is not the night that kills, it is the frost."*[6]

As Paul wrote:

> *Do I make my plans like a worldly man, ready to say Yes and No at once? As surely as God is faithful, our word to you has not been Yes and No. For the Son of God, Jesus Christ, whom we preached among you, Silvanus and Timothy and I, was not Yes and No, but in him it is always Yes. For all the promises of God find their Yes in him. For all the promises of God find their Yes in him. That is why we utter the Amen through him, to the glory of God. But it is God who establishes us with you in Christ, and has commissioned us; he has put his seal upon us and given us his Spirit in our hearts as a guarantee.*[7]

---

6. Miguel de Unamuno, *The Tragic Sense of Life*, (New York: Harcourt, 1971), 14.

7. 2 Corinthians 1:17–22.

2

"Can We Live with Promise?"

Hosea 11:1–13; Romans 12:3–13

COMMONS

Have we truly opened ourselves, and opened our common life, to the promises of God?

We were raised in the heart of a modest village, poor in things and rich in soul, forty years ago and just before the end of the Christian era. That village was arranged, and nicely so, around a commons, a town square. You can walk today, undisturbed because the town is empty, across the length of the common ground at the heart of the village. On Thursdays the high school band plays, two of three flutes keeping the right time, and a tired band director, still gay in a town that does not admit the existence of the category, and a loud drum. Sit for a minute on the bench, read a paper. Watch the light spill through the fountain. Have a cup of coffee. We have time. It's Sunday! Your mind wanders, as during a meandering sermon.

Here our children made their first dollars, selling bracelets at the Saturday market. Here 150 years ago Colgate was founded by thirteen men with thirteen dollars. Here in 1861 men from Sherburne and Earlville mustered and marched to the Utica train. Some came home four years later. Here Andy Rooney waited in 1941 to take a bus to New York and WWII. He did come home, changed. Hear the town gathered and later went to church to pray on November 22, 1963. Here we spent our wedding night.

The botched development of suburban America has left out town squares, and more generally any commons at all, other than the road and the mall, our witness to the gods of motion and consumption. We have fled for the hills, and the comfort and isolation of curbless streets. The town square has been eclipsed and repressed, almost everywhere, except behind the faces and masks of our daily selves. There, inside, lurks a love of the commons, and a hunger to live the free promise of God. I am trying to describe the topography of your souls, folks. A church bell here, a town square there - they represent the best of your emerging salvation, you wild children of the dream! Watch for the return of the repressed.

Common ground, and the town square commons, comes from a deep English tradition, centuries old, biblical and fierce in its old love of freedom, a tradition that protected the rights of the many by providing common space. On the commons, as in baptism and eucharist, all are equal and all are precious and all are free. See - an older couple, buying apples. See—three boys on scooters. See—teenagers, holding hands, gazing down, growing and beautiful. See—there you are!—speaking with another, as I to Thou. The town square is common ground, space glorious space, open to life and love and the other. Yes, a few have already guessed the next move…

The architectural form of common ground is the church. The literal and metaphorical space of the church is quintessentially the location of precious love and precious freedom. Salvation is about space. In my Father's house there are many rooms. As far as the east is from the west, so far does he remove our transgressions. There is a wideness to divine mercy, as wide as the sea. The church is the space opened by the invasion of what the prophets called *hesed*, covenant love, *hesed*, common love, *hesed*.

A COVENANT LOVE

In the eighth century before Christ, as the kingdoms of Ephraim and Judah collapsed under the weight of external attack, the divine voice was heard first through Amos and then through Hosea.

Hosea understood his own personal life as an incarnation of God's redeeming love. Do we have the courage to see our pain and glory in the same light? For Hosea, the ministry was the message. Do we hear the words our deeds utter? In Hosea, redemption comes with a price. Do we dare to pay the price of promise?

Hosea took a wife named Gomer. What a name. Gomer became a prostitute, not only leaving and cuckolding her husband, but bearing children to him who were not his. He named the first Jezreel, a reminder of blood. The second he named, "Not pitied." The third he named "Not my people." But though Gomer broke the very marrow of the bone of promise, Hosea, bitter and angry though he was, continued painstakingly to pursue her, in a life, like yours, laden with love and anger. Hosea kept the covenant promise even though Gomer had not only broken it, but had abused, misused and dishonored the same promise. Isn't that astounding? Hosea, in the teeth of rejection, continued tenderly to love a harlot.

This is why. Hosea understood his ministry and life as a personal incarnation of the God's redeeming love. Did God promise to love? So would Hosea. Did God keep the covenant promise? So would Hosea. Did God persevere in love, in the face of human rejection? So would Hosea. Did God continue to love, though his beloved loved others actively and with a willingness to hurt? So would Hosea.

Hosea the prophet deplored his nation's harlotry, even as he persevered in steadfast love. He kept faith with the promise of a better day. He kept faith with the promise of a better day. Do we?

Years ago, our church was daily cared for by a retired woman, quite a successful business woman in her own right, who served as our housekeeper, and by hook and crook kept the church clean, overseeing the sextons, hectoring the pastors, scowling at the children. She especially watched the younger boys. They knew better than to unpack the daycare toys on Sunday and pull out the soccer ball for use on the newly waxed fellowship floor. Iva would be on the lookout. Iva would tend and care, pursue and love, even in the face of their rejection. One Sunday, the boys got loose. They found the ball and began to play, wisely posting a lookout at the door. One of the boys, the youngest, was the new kid on the block, son of a recently arrived assistant pastor. Suddenly, Iva was spotted. The boys ran for their lives, like Bobby Knight leaving Bloomington. The new kid stood in the middle of the floor, holding the ball, and wondering about the mass exodus. "Ben", I said, "what happened to him?" "Oh, Dad," said Ben, a wise man of eight years of age, "it was awful." "Awful?" "When Iva came, it was awful." "What happened to him?" "All I can say Dad was that he was, he was . . . *Ivatized*."

Relentless pursuit, persevering love, the daily reception of the covenant promise-this is the gospel of Hosea.

ONE SPIRIT, ONE BODY

In Jesus Christ, a new day has dawned, the better day has come. Not "might come." Not "could come." Not "should come if we would do better." Not "has a chance to come." In Christ, there is a new creation. Now. Promised and delivered. Present. *Hic et nunc.*

The promises of God, which find their yes in Christ, make of us one body, with many members, guided by one spirit, of many gifts.

St. Paul exhorts us to *love one another, genuinely*. It is remarkable how easy it can be in life and faith to forget the main point. God is at work in the world to make and keep human life human. We are human when we receive and give love.

Spiritually, the best thing for the minister about vacation is the chance to go to worship and sit in the pew and pray and sing, and fish around for money for the collection. In a smaller church, with a weaker choir and a minimal staff—but right there is the promise of a space for real life. Worship is the single most humanizing moment and hour in the week. We are bathed again in our own humanity.

Listen for the way Paul invariably calls his people to live in the promise of God. Spacious is God's grace: we are members of one body. Spacious is God's grace: we are indebted to one Spirit. Spacious is God's grace: we are set free to be free, and inspired by love to love. Spacious is God's grace: spacious is God's grace.

AN OPEN LIFE

Beloved, if God has so loved us, then we also should love one another. If God has granted us such space, such running room, then we too should be spacious in our open living with others.

There is a clean wind blowing through our lives. Let us drive with the top down and enjoy it! There is a loving presence promised us. Let us open the front door and greet it! All the promises of God are fulfilled in Christ! Let us live the promise.

Asbury First is one of the few, perhaps one of the last county-wide town squares in our region. People come here, drawn by the precious love and precious freedom of the commons here. Since 1995 this church has grown by 20%. People are turning out to walk the village park, and to enjoy the space of God. There is a longing, lodged in our subconscious selves, for genuine community. We grope and hunt for spaces in which freely to love, to live the promise. In our time, let us expand the circle of love, rebuild the village green, and make wide the portals of heaven! Someone did so for us. It is the least we can do.

Someone gave us a weightless freedom. We have learned to float, like a beginner swimmer. We are space walkers, like Mr. Lu from Webster walking in outer space, hand in hand with an enemy.

It may take time. Vaclav Havel, 40 years a dissident, 30 years a playwright, 20 years an activist, 10 years in prison, still *lived the promise*. Now he is the freely elected president of a free Checkoslovakia. "Hope gives us the strength to live and continually to try new things, even in conditions that seem hopeless . . . Without hope it is impossible to live with dignity and meaning."

As Lincoln said, "(Before Gettysburg) I felt my own weakness and lack of power knew that if the country was to be saved, it was because he willed it. When I went down from my room I felt that there could be no doubt of the issue. The burden seemed to have trolled off my shoulders, my intense anxiety was relieved and in its place came a great sense of trust, and that was why I did not doubt the result at Gettysburg."

I wonder. Can we live, truly live, with the spacious, mighty promise of God? Can we conform our own lives and our church life to such spacious hope? Can we welcome the hurting and touch the hurt with the hand of Christ? Spiritual and actual space for such welcoming are at the heart of our ministry.

NORTH STAR

I was witness, once, to such promissory and spacious welcome. I remember one autumn, when a young man from our community went north to St. Lawrence College. Somehow it happened as the cold fell, he fell ill. He contracted meningitis, was misdiagnosed, and died. Eddie was a football player, a musician, and had been our patrol leader. He was a model for the younger kids. His dad was not a churchgoer. Like many, he had serious and creditable objections to organized religion. But I remember one night, let us imagine it a bright harvest moon night, with the North Star gleaming, seeing him walk toward the back porch and knock at our door. In he came, smoking a pipe. And there at the kitchen table, on a crisp starlit autumn night, I overheard a conversation that ultimately landed me in the ministry. At midlife I realize in hindsight that this simple promissory conversation, overheard from the next room, more than any other, convinced me of the priority of ministry, the place where we talk about love and death.

The two men sat at the table and smoked pipes in silence, a silence thunderous with the heart shout anger of loss, with the cry of the heart in the face of inexplicable tragedy, with the heavy emptiness of loss.

What do you say to a man who has lost his son?
"Would you like some pie, Ed?"
"Pie is good."
More silence and more and more.
"Coffee and pie—good on a cool night."
"How about some cheese?"
"Cheese is good."
More silence and more and more.
"Another slice Ed?"
"Another slice is good."
More silence and more and more.
Now the pipes again, and spoons rattling in the coffee cups.
"How is it Ed?"
"Ah, you know . . ."
More silence. The silence of two men talking about death and love.
"I guess I'll have a little more pie Marcia."
"Pie is good. And this is good pie."

In an open space, with the welcome of an open door, with a sense of promise drawing one and guiding the other, two men didn't talk about love and death. There was a long and smokey silence and then a rustle of chairs, and a prayer.

> *O Lord support us all the day long of this troublous life*
> *Until the shadows lengthen*
> *And the evening comes*
> *And the busy world is hushed*
> *And the fever of life is over*

And our work is done
Then in thy mercy
Grant us a safe rest, a happy lodging and peace at the last.

3

"Can Promise Emerge from a Land of Plenty?"

Amos 5:21–25; Romans 2:12–16

A LOOK INTO THE LIBRARY

I WONDER: IS OUR 'God' too small? Have we fully appreciated the divine compassion for the needy, God's protective preference for the poor?

Walk for a moment back to the heart of life, that for which your soul yearns. A church bell rings. A village green beckons. Across the street you can see a library, an old house converted to stacks of books. Today the library hums with the quiet conversation of the saints their watch keeping, to hear the night of weeping become the morn of song. Today we return books that are overdue, with the current fine of 8 cents per day per book. 40 years ago, in this town, the chief civic fundraiser, which built a hospital and a ballpark and too, this little library, was an annual book sale. Every autumn, on one October day when the weather was still warm, the school let out at noon, the businesses closed at noon, and the town swarmed to the library and adjacent lots and buildings to buy each other's books. I see *The Hobbit, Harriet the Spy, Tom Sawyer, A Wrinkle in Time*. The adults bought each other's dog-eared volumes, and skimmed along reading by way of each other's underlined paragraphs. Someone else had cut the trail. Why not follow?

In the library, out in the center of the room, you can see a large dictionary on a revolving stand. Let's walk over, and pick up the magnifying glass, and browse for a minute. (Glasses?) *Is . . . Sex . . . Juniper, junk, Jupiter . . . ah, Justice: "the principle of moral rightness, equity."*

THE PROPHET REMEMBERS THE POOR

Our spiritual library, a collection of 66 volumes, is the Bible. And in the older room, back in the second stack, just around the corner from Law, we find a collection of prophets, starting in 750 BC with Amos.

Amos was an unlearned shepherd boy from Tekoa, a small town in the north. I wonder if Tekoa had a library, and I wonder if Amos was a regular there. Maybe. Amos looked at the plenty of his people, and found it a mile wide and an inch deep. He was gardener, specializing in the trimming of Sycamore trees, and of course he had his sheep. He had time to think. I wonder what he would think of our last decade: a tripled stock market, a booming economy, new internet commerce, expanding portfolios. I wonder what he would thing of our last decade: curiosities about worship modes, tunes for singing, alternative settings.

At a party last spring we met a couple who have a daughter and son-in-law in California. The parents cannot fathom their children! The young couple are dual professionals in San Francisco, frenetically busy and successfully prosperous. Their net worth already—and they are not yet 30—is more than $1M. But they are anxious to retire soon, and they feel competitively and comparatively poor, when they measure against their coworkers. Somehow they sense that they are missing the bus. What is it that truly gnaws at them? Is it concern for security? Or is, down in the caverns of the soul, rather the sense of broken promises, sleeping at the bottom of our opulent rivers of life?

Jon Voight wakes up sweating at the end of *Deliverance,* because he sees a hand emerging from underwater. The hand of promise, promise broken past and promise kept future, is going to emerge, sometime, in our history.

To a similarly opulent and religious people Amos, alone, hearing God's word spoke God's word:

> *Take away from me the noise of your church music*
> *To the melody of your instruments I will not listen*

> *But let justice roll down like waters*
> *And righteousness as an ever flowing stream.*[1]

Intimacy with the God of Amos and Jesus is not to be established or maintained through hymnody, a word hard for a singing Methodist like me to hear. There is chumminess, a coziness to our God talk and song that ignores God's sovereignty, and God's claim on human obedience. In age of flat religion, churches without sanctuaries, worship spaces without height—just here is Amos with a high word, *justice*.

After all, God had established a covenant. Noah, Abraham, Moses, David. For the people of faith, life may have meaning as it is an expression of the emerging promise, the will of God, especially tested by the way a people treats those who are voiceless, shoeless, clueless. The unnoticed. We become so caught up in our own life project that we risk forgetting the least, the last, the lost. Until, at last, we are brought up short. There is a day reserved for the bringing up short of those long on religion and plenty—me and you. Are we living in hope that the Day of God, the day of justice, the day of righteousness will come to an end so that cheating and exploitation can resume (Heschel)? Is this what lurks behind our current openness—listen to the autumn's political debates—to gambling, to building local economies 90 minutes east and 90 minutes west, on games of chance and the fecklessness of our citizenry? I thought I read something in our Book of Discipline about the corrupting influence of gambling. The divine delight arises from justice. The divine desire is prior to whatever may currently have become legal. What is legal is not simply and only what is right and just.

PAUL PROMISES THE RELIABILITY OF CONSCIENCE

In Jesus Christ, according to the Apostle Paul, we are given a lasting, everflowing stream of connection to the divine justice. This is good news, though sometimes it may not feel so. Paul names the invasion of Christ, just here, with the word *conscience*. He asserts that we all have a conscience, religious and unreligious both. And he makes his assertion "according to my good news." It is the same voice, inner voice, intimate inner voice, on which the prophet Amos relied, to which Paul directs us today. This, for Paul, is the best of good news. The voice of the prophet, now again then again, emerges in the promise of Jesus Christ, an ever-flowing stream.

---

1. Amos 5.23–24.

Perhaps conscience is relegated to the back pew, to the periphery, to the subway walls and tenement halls, to the still listening young. Still, conscience lives.

A while ago, I asked a college junior, one of my best students, what he was doing after graduation. He thought for a while and then said, "I would like to volunteer for a year, but my parents want me to get a job or study more." I listened and nodded and thought: *Go Parents. Yes: job, study. One for our side.* Driving home, though, like Amos among the sycamores and sheep, I had a little forced time to think. As I thought, I became truly ashamed. Paul described the life of the conscience, and my student voiced his conscience. *I want to volunteer. I want to give to others. I want to seek the right. I want to work for justice. I want promise to emerge in this land of plenty and I feel the promise of God on my still open, young heart.* Yes, I had implied with a wink and a nod, sure. But let's face it. Your parents are right.

Are they? Are we? Was I?

The voice of prophetic promise lives, but it is muted, left on the sidelines, given over to the young, ignored.

Paul of Tarsus, Paul of the letter to Philemon, Paul of Romans 13, Paul of the ongoing collection for the poor, Paul of Romans 14 and the strong and weak—the Apostle asserts the ever flowing righteousness embedded in your conscience. You have a conscience both to accuse and to excuse, and so do I. Is this good news? *"Disturbance of the soul, restless murmuring, cavil, and protest: such may be signposts to the peace of God which passes all understanding."*[2] God sets upon us all the same just expectation and the same emerging promise. Just consult your conscience. Let your conscience be your guide.

THE PROMISE OF JUSTICE TODAY

One looks back over the past lucrative decade in this, the land of the free and the home of the brave, and one wonders.

What if, along this opulent river, our mantra had been not "economy, stupid" but "theonomy, dear." Not the law of the household but the divine law?

What if, over ten years, our nation had been harnessed to the explosive dream of liberty and justice, *for all?*

2. Barth.

What if our personal lives, across America, had been forged like steel in a white heat of compunction, reverence, self-discipline, frugality and generosity?

What if, in this ten year season of gain (a tripled stock market, a world-wide webbed economy, and rocketing portfolios all around), we had been led by a vision of a great dream, of justice and liberty, *for all?*

We get the leadership we deserve. But what if we had seen the river of wealth across this land as a great surge toward justice?

What if, in this smooth season, the harsh voice of Amos had been heard?

What if we had not settled, this last decade, for liberty and *charity* for all?

What if, in our time of ease, we had affirmed demanding leaders, strongly compassionate leaders, of the stature of Washington and Lincoln and Roosevelt? If Roosevelt made a river in the desert of the '30's, what would he have been able to do with the 90's? If Lincoln brought the waters of union in the dust of the civil war, what could he have done with the complacent opulence of the 90's? If Washington could forge a nation in the cold ice of Valley Forge, what could he have done with the sunny, steaming fantastic wealth of Silicon Valley?

A great watershed of prosperity has cascaded down upon this country. I recognize that not all of us have been drenched. For some it has been a sprinkle in time. But what as a nation have we made of it?

At the time of our greatest success and excess, we have frittered away precious time and precious money on personal pleasure, and our leaders, in high office and elsewhere, have cut the trail.

What if we had not studied the dictionary definitions of "is" and "sex," our focus so present tense and so personally pleasurable, and instead had looked into the J column, standing in the poor library of our heart of hearts, and grappled with *mishpat and dikaiosune*, justice and righteousness?

We forget the 10% of our people who have been left behind, at the very time when our resources could have allowed us stunningly to defeat poverty.

In southern Madison County today there are very few dentists because there are very few teeth.

In our weaker schools, there are very few excellent teachers because there are very few ordered, safe, disciplined, respectful classes.

In our pulpits, there are very few true voices, because in our pews we are sated with comfort, and no longer hunger and thirst for *misphat, dikaiosune, justice*.

Promise can emerge in a land of plenty, when none are left behind, no not one.

This August, I backed out of the driveway and nearly hit a finely dressed, six foot, gray haired, distinguished gentleman. He carried a nice brown sweater, carefully folded over his arm. He had no idea where he was, lost in the forest of Alzheimer's disease, sure his wife was just around the corner, though he had been walking alone for three hours.

Promise can emerge in plenty, when justice prevails.

Suppose, for a moment, we had all the best qualities of our presidential candidates and none of their weaknesses. Nader's utopian idealism, without any tendency to anarchy. Gore's sincere populism, without the repugnant mendacity, the moral relativism of his boss. Bush's lone star and high hat optimism, without regressive tax policy. Buchanan's openness to life, without the disdain for others who maintain, with St. Augustine, a respectful agnosticism about such ultimate issues. We need the best of all these men, and others. But that misses the point! That misses the main truth! If we had all this, it wouldn't add up to 10% of the promise that is smoldering in our well being, the promise that is seething in our prosperity, the promise that is about to emerge from our plenty.

Let justice roll down like waters . . .

Our 'God', as J. B. Phillips said, has become too small. No. We missed our chance in the 1990's. We will have to start over. And starting over is hard. Ask anybody who took a new job this week, or who went to AA for the first time, or who moved from one pulpit to another this summer. We will have to start over, and look again at the soul library definition of *justice*.

NORTH STAR

In August we stood one night on the western edge of our country, at the San Francisco Bay. It is a beautiful, even a majestic set of vistas. We happened to be standing in Oakland, looking out at the summer sky, admiring, among other stars, Polaris, the North and promise star. We had finished a delicious dinner with a dear friend, who herself has had to start all over this year. It is hard to start over. To pack and unpack. To unsettle and settle. To leave the comfort of dozens of friends and, like a freshman in college or a camper in July, to walk to the dining hall alone.

When it comes to justice, when it comes to the poor, we as country will need to start over. That is hard.

4

"A Grain of Truth"

Amos 7:7–17; Galatians 2:1–5

POST OFFICE

Picture for a moment the outline of a simple village green. To the left there stands a church, its bells ringing again with a Sunday invitation, a call to the living to hear something of the meaning of life: in your soul those bells ring too. To the right, a library stands in tribute to the power of words: your soul hungers for a word fitly spoken. Across the expanse green there is space, gracious space: in the soul's back reaches there opens out such a free, loving meadow too. If you turn—well you can turn any direction you want, after all, this is your imagination at work, not mine—you spy a depression era Post Office, once upon a time the communications center of village life: man does not live by bread alone, murmurs the soul.

They leave the Post Office open over the weekend, now, so that if you need stamps or post cards you can buy them. You take them and leave the money in a little brown box marked "money." Isn't that a great way to mark a money box? "Money." The soul delights in such a pre-millennial simplicity, dating from the days when we did know what words meant (words like "is," "sex," "justice," "welcome"). We have a few little examples left in church. We call the collection plates the collection plates, not "giving opportunity baskets." We call pledge Sunday, "pledge Sunday", not "community enhancement day." We call tithing, tithing, not "proportional dedication practice." Like the old village post office, and like your soul, the church has not yet ascended to the Olympian heights of post—Christian newspeak.

In the early 1960's we received mail the old way, without a computer. This, as I recall, included envelopes sealed with tongues and kisses, stamps selected for collector value, handwritten addresses, posted post haste or no haste and you could tell the difference, sometimes, later, perfume scents and hints, and a return address. Every autumn, without fail, there came a birthday card, with a Rochester return address, spelled out in laborious print: *30 Lilac Drive*. The post office promised and delivered, as does the spirit of love and freedom even today. Within the envelope there rode a birthday check made out to the number of years for that year's celebration. I realized that if I lived long enough I would be a rich man. That is still true. My aunt's consistent, dependable, regular, loving communication arrived on the village green every autumn. Preaching is the communication of truth through personality. The church is the community of truth. The gospel is truth. As Karl Barth said, the minister is a mailman. Deliva de letta de soona de betta. May our souls receive an epistle of truth every now and then, sealed with a kiss. For though we are living in the Age of Deception, there is a self-correcting spirit of truth, loose in the universe.

PLUMB LINE

Truth hurts. That is how we know it is the truth. Humorously my dear son Ben recalls his first summer in Rochester. We had heard that Wegmans hired all the teenagers here, and sent them to college for free. So we sent Ben off for indentured servitude, a bicycle ride away. He spent the summer parking carts, bagging melons, registering purchases. One day Bob Dimarco took Ben aside. Bob is the assistant manager in the store. "Ben, do you see the line of sixteen registers?" Yes Bob. "Do you see how straight the line is?" Yes Bob. "Do you see how the workers are all dressed with their ties straight?" Yes Bob. "Do you see how their aprons are all clean and tied at the back in a bow knot?" Yes Bob. "Do you see how they all work in rhythm, efficiently and happily." Yes Bob. Then Bob paused for effect, and Ben paused in telling for fuller effect, and I pause for fuller effect still. He said: "I don't see that in you Ben!"

My friend says only your boss and spouse will tell you the truth. Once upon a village green he might have included your preacher. Real religion, for Amos and Paul and you, is never very far from truth.

Amos was called to heel by the court prophet Amaziah, who decried Amos' criticism of Israel:

Amos you country bumpkin. You unlearned, unpatriotic, unpolished hooligan. You embarrassment to God and man both. How dare you assert such harsh negativity about religious and political leaders? Who died and left you boss? If you are so smart why are you not rich? No longer tell us about defeat coming, about the king dying, about exile around the corner, about sons and daughters slaughtered, about unclean graves to sleep in, about trouble.

But Amos took a plumb line, the builder's measure of truth, and said only this: "Thus says the Lord: I am setting a plumb line in the midst of my people." The body, they may kill. God's truth abideth still. The devil, Belial, is the father of lies.

May we notice that Amos predicts a return to slavery. The Bible is about God's promise of freedom, and our perennial penchant for rechaining ourselves. The ultimate outcome of falsehood, though it takes a generation to emerge, is slavery.

I set a plumb line in their midst. What is plumb, what is true, will last, and what is not, will not.

GOSPEL TRUTH

I have an old friend, now blind and ornery at 97, who said very little about religion in the years I knew him. He built houses for a living—beautiful homes. In his evenings he bought church campgrounds, built chapels, prepared Sunday School lessons, served on umpteen church committees. He had a gift for building the infrastructure to support community life. He built living rooms, as he said, "so that when the boy comes to pick up his date they have someplace nice to sit." He built sanctuaries that, as he said, "spelled church when you walked in." He built secular and religious summer camps for kids who, as he said, "came from nothing like I did." Rarely did I hear him speak about his faith. Only twice, in all those years of faithfulness, do I remember him to lift out a spiritual comment. These are people you like to listen to when they talk about truth. You listen when they occasionally speak. Once he said, during one of the seasonal religious fundamentalist monsoons to which our denomination seems particularly prone, "I know the Bible is important, but I think some people read it wrong." That is another sermon. Another time he said, "You know, for some reason telling the truth for some people is a long day of real hard work." That is this sermon. Truth eludes us if we are not vigilant and diligent.

After laboring alone for fourteen years, Paul of Tarsus went to Jerusalem for what we now call the Jerusalem Council. Some twenty years after the cross and resurrection of Christ, Paul the apostle to the non-Jews went to confer with the mother church, Peter and James and all. How paltry are the little comments read earlier! What we would give now to know what happened in the city of Jerusalem about 48 CE, as the varieties of earliest Christianity met together, Jew and Greek, male and female, slave and free, Paul and Peter. Luke in the book of Acts presents later an entirely sanitized version of the story, perhaps holding no more information than we heard earlier this morning. In fact, though Paul clearly says in our passage this morning that Titus, a Greek, was not required to be circumcised, Luke in Acts 15, in order to cover over the earlier conflict, circumcises dear Titus. Literarily not actually. Paul fought "those of repute in Jerusalem." He fought Peter in Antioch. He fought his Galatian competitor teachers in this letter. What for? I repeat that we are in the birth canal of our faith with this letter that birth like all births, occurring with violence. What is all the shouting about? Says Paul, "That the truth of the gospel might be preserved for you."[1] Such a stark phrase, "the truth of the gospel." Such an uncompromising phrase, "the truth of the gospel." Such a plumb line of a phrase, "the truth of the gospel." Paul composes a whole letter in which the content of Jesus Christ is the revelation of truth.

Do you find it humbling to recall how often the Christian church has turned a deaf ear to truth, to Amos and to Paul? Our daughter's first college play was about Galileo, forced to recant what was true. Or think of Martin Luther's friends, saying, in effect, "Yes, it is so, but could you not become a little more accommodating, a little more collegial, a little more pacific?" What of the Scopes trial, a humble teacher browbeaten over an expression of truth, attacked with, of all things, the Bible? Even in the church, espe-

---

1. Galatians 2:5.

cially for the church, the truth takes time to emerge. But the truth will out. There is a self-correcting spirit of truth that is loose in the universe.

TRUTH VS. ORDER TODAY

What good news this is for us!

For seven decades, religion and truth were muzzled in the Soviet Union. Yet Alexander Solzenitsyn and others practiced religion and bore witness to truth. Before *glasnost* and *perestroika*, he wrote, "the world demands of us a spiritual blaze and a constant vigilance in defense of truth." You may fear that wayward regimes never die. They do. There is a self-correcting spirit of truth, loose in the universe.

In the same period, Czheckoslovakia wallowed in the dungeon of untruth. But Vaclav Havel, forty years a dissident, thirty years a playwrite, twenty years an activist, and ten years in prison, practiced his agnosticism and spoke the truth. Today the poet is the freely elected President of a free land! You may fear falsehood empowered never falls. Fear not. There is a self-correcting spirit of truth, loose in the universe.

For almost 500 years, Protestants have shrugged with dismay at the untruths within Roman Catholicism (the celibacy of the priesthood, the sacrifice of the mass, the infallibility of the Pope, and the sub-ordination of women). Will truth ever again connect us to our Roman sisters and brothers? Now along comes Garry Wills, a Roman Catholic historian, has written a book this year called *Papal Sin: Structures of Deceit*. He argues that while Medieval popes succumbed to the sin of avarice, modern popes have been overcome by deceit. Untruth! About what? The celibacy of the priesthood, the sacrifice of the mass, the infallibility of the Pope, the subordination of women. You may fear that religious authority is unaccountable. Fear not. There is a self-correcting spirit of truth, loose in the universe.

Of course, the comfortable way to read his book as a Methodist is to acclaim the criticisms of Rome that we prideful Protestants have long known. The less comfortable way is to realize that his argument fits us too, by extension. There are some things we just have a hard time saying to one another, in our denomination. You make your list, and send it to me this week. You may fear that our church has preferred order to truth, with regard to persons of homosexual orientation, and that our reluctance to recommend has spilled over into an unwillingness to accept. You may fear that the masculinist, conservative, interest in order and old morality may ever prevail. Fear not. There is a self-correcting spirit of truth, loose in the universe.

Or on the other hand, you may fear that our church has preferred liberty to life, with regard to the issue of choice. Perhaps you affirm our Book of Discipline and its protection of the mother's freedom, and yet you also recognize other, lingering, haunting features of veracity—the fate of the pre-born, the condition of the culture, the role of the father. And you may fear that the feminist, liberal interest in ideology and power may ever prevail. Fear not. There is a self-correcting spirit of truth, loose in the universe.

And what of our country? Chris read to me from the *Federalist Papers* the other night, that wise and promising set of documents outlining a government meant to avoid both the dangers of King George and the dangers of the French Revolution. James Madison had an ear for truth. Do we? Perhaps you wonder, "Do we care anymore whether our chief executive lies to us? What kind of accountability can there be when the power of high office is used mendaciously, and then not called to account? In August of 1998, the military might of the United States of America was used to bomb two spots, one in Afghanistan and one in the Sudan. We were fighting terrorism with those bombs, remember? We killed two camels and burned down a pharmacy. We never heard if anyone died. Oh, did I mention that those bombs were dropped during the week of Mr. Clinton's further false testimony about his earlier false testimony? Do we care whether we are lied to? Do we care whether unsuspecting Muslims die to further the project of such a lie? Who have we become?" But look! I submit that the politics of this autumn, from all sides, has taken a much more serious look at truth. Fear not. There is a self-correcting spirit of truth, loose in the universe.

LONDON BROIL

This pulpit was constructed out of a respect for truth. For a long time, I thought that the many best and brightest ministers who have left for other vocations, did so to have more free time, more money, more status. Now I wonder whether our capacity to tell the truth, or our lack of truth telling has frightened away those bright and sensitive souls who might well have weathered all the regular indignities of ministry, but for whom a truthless time proved too much. I need fear. There is a self-correcting spirit of truth, loose in the universe, that over time again will fill our pulpits.

From the Atlantic to the Pacific, we have voices of courage and truth to inspire us. Let us affirm those who, at cost to themselves, lovingly and consistently tell the truth. You will know them by their manner of discourse, as well as their substance. The envelope counts too, with its return address, and perfumed scent, and sealing with tongue and kiss. From Hyannisport to Oakland and back, the voices have been there.

In Hyannisport, beneath the North Star at night, you can see the park and monument devoted to Jack Kennedy. There with scores of sailboats bobbing at their slips, a short little line is chiseled in the stone:

I believe that America should set sail and not merely lie still in the harbor.

For here is our grain of truth: born in a manger, raised in the outback, matured in a carpenters' home, who preached and taught and healed, who wrote nothing and said everything, and who suffered so that in our suffering we might be loved, and who died, so that in our dying we might be saved.

5

"A Promise of Freedom and Love"

"Age to Age: The Church Family Gathers"

Hosea 6:4–6; Matthew 9:9–13

A VILLAGE CHURCH

Down deeper than usually we want to swim in the dark pool of the subconscious and the soul there are saving longings for grace, rising up and taking ownership of the visible world. Imagine an ample village green. Church bells chime. Children enter a library. With cane in hand, a woman deposits a letter at the Post Office. We wander in the meadow, the commons, the gracious space of freedom and love, and now pause to knock at the humble door of a Methodist Church. No one is inside. We are alone before the simple altar and pulpit, and in sight of a stained glass window of Jesus, knocking, knocking, knocking with lantern in hand, knocking at the door of the soul. Below him there lies open a Bible, like the one on our altar, and like the ones we present today.

What is the Bible about? It is a question children and adults can both ask. The Bible is a pond shallow enough for toddlers to wade in, and deep enough to drown an elephant. What is the Bible about?

A PROMISE OF FREEDOM: HOSEA

In the first place, the Bible is a book about freedom, or better, a library of books about freedom, divine and human. God is loving us into love and freeing us into freedom. It is freedom that is born, with heartache, in the Garden of Eden. It is freedom that is restored, with blessing, in the covenant with Abraham. It is freedom that is promised, through famine, to the brothers of Joseph. It is freedom that lies across the Red Sea, as Israel flees Pharaoh. Deborah sings a song of freedom! It is freedom that Moses glimpses, as he dies, sitting atop Mt. Nebo. It is freedom that Samuel desires, and Saul denigrates, and David defends, and Solomon defines.

It is freedom that Israel loses, when she ignores the prophets, and freedom that is resurrected by Cyrus who frees Israel from Babylon. It is freedom to worship the One God, with whom Jacob wrestled as Israel (one who wrestles with God), for which the Temple was restored. And it is freedom that Israel awaited as Israel awaited Messiah. In the first place, the Bible is a book about freedom. So when the Bible is used in ways that increase slavery and decrease freedom, beware. In those cases, even in our time, the teaching about the Bible is unbiblical.

John Wesley used the Bible to free coal miners from poverty. Abraham Lincoln used the Bible to free African Americans from slavery. Walter Rauschenbush used the Bible to free immigrants from destitution. Georgia Harkness used the Bible to free women from narrowed roles. Martin Luther King used the Bible to free blacks from segregation. Today many read in Galatians a further freedom of homosexuals from exclusion, and a further freedom of the pre-born from extinction.

Still, the freedom in the Bible comes with a high price, a heavy cost. For all the plaudits great leaders receive, freedom breaks out, one by one, heart by heart. So Hosea, heartsick over his lost love, imagined a similar divine grace, and roared: "I desire mercy, not sacrifice, the knowledge of God, not burnt offerings."[1]

The prophets recall for us the divine desire that all, all might be included in the great open space of covenant love. It is this great promise of freedom that opens and closes the Bible, and that empowers men and women to get up in the morning and to face insurmountable odds, and unwinnable battles, and lost causes. Some causes are worth fighting for even though the outcome is foredoomed.

---

1. Hosea 6:6.

A PROMISE OF LOVE: MATTHEW

In the second place, the Bible is a book about love, or better, a library of books about love, divine and human. God is freeing us into freedom and loving us into love. It is love that Jesus teaches as the measure of all activity. "But I say to you, love your enemies, and pray for those who persecute you."[2] It is love that Paul names as the presence of God in Christ to him. "The life I now live in the flesh I live by the faith of the Son of God who loved me and gave himself up for me."[3] It is love that John commends as our only experience of God. "Beloved let us love one another for love is of God and one who loves is born of God and knows God for God is Love."[4]

Matthew takes up the line from Hosea, placing on the lips of Jesus a great Greek verb, "thelo". We are told: go and *learn* what this means. A clue is given that Jesus has given the old verse a new spin. And indeed, in Matthew's hands, he has. Here is the meaning of this word, thelo: I desire, I delight in, I enjoy, I crave, I hunger for, I long for . . . Love is something we receive before it becomes the freedom we achieve.

Love is the power that operates to keep us whole when life splinters us into fragments. God is love at work to encourage us through illness. God is love at work to befriend us in loneliness. God is love at work to maintain us in sorrow. God is love at work to restore us from hate. God is love at work to forgive us our sin. We know love in retrospect.

I remember sitting in church one summer many years ago. The church was Trinity Church in Auburn, then and now an old, worn out building, supported, then and now, by an aged congregation. The choir consisted of three sopranos and one alto, singing "In the Garden." It was a hot August day. The sermon, in retrospect, in form and content was awful. Like the peace of God, it passed all understanding and endured forever. Yet, I hold that sermon, that lifeless malformed misfire of a rhetorical blemish, to have been the saving word of God. It was about forgiveness. That is all I remember. I doubt I knew, entering the worn out sanctuary, how much I needed such a word. If the word depended upon the skill of the servant of the word, I would have heard nothing. But God speaks God's word, and God can use a dead dog to speak if God so chooses. I suppose I am not the only twenty year old ever to have needed forgiveness. Perhaps you know

2. Matt 5:44.
3. Galatians 2:20.
4. 1 John 4:7–8.

another. Perhaps you are another. If so, may God's love be at work in your heart to mend you, for God is a pardoning God (Wesley).

And pardon is God's work. God does not need us to do God's work of pardoning love.

AN INVITATION

As our Bibles are presented today, let us dust them off, scrub them clean, read them closely, and peruse them under the bifocal promise of freedom and love.

6

"Don't Get Too Comfortable!"

Micah 6:6–8; 1 Corinthians 7:25–31

THE VILLAGE GREEN FIVE AND DIME

If you have some change in your pocket come with me for a minute. We are going into the village green five and ten-cent store, to see what we can see. Don't you love this little store? For fifty years—even more—the shop has somehow survived, meeting the essential impermanent desires of the day. Here you buy pencils and notebooks for school, a scarf in the winter, a squirt gun in the spring, a yo-yo for summer, and come autumn again, something to wear at Halloween. John Wesley said his English people were "a nation of shopkeepers." So in our region, the small business, farm, store provide our backbone. The same scents and smells linger here, from so long ago: a mixture of newsprint and bubble gum and paint and perfume. The uncovered tongue and groove wooden floor creeks in the same odd places.

For so many years this store was the stage on which its owner performed. He wore a handlebar mustache, bright white hair, a stunning smile, and cackled with a child's laugh. He looked like the Wizard of Oz. Years later, when I sat next to him as a fellow Rotarian, he looked the same—the Wizard of Oz. His little world of tiny transactions, most of the purchases made by people who had to reach up to the counter, on tiptoe, somehow kept his soul lit. Of all people, I guess, he could have had the most reason to doubt his role. His customers were few and supported only by weekly allowances. The transactions involved pennies and dimes. The days were long, the hours demanding. But the sun streaming through his clean window touched most often a smiling, happy face. I can remember handing over some little coin in exchange for some little trinket. In that little sunlight, over the exchange of impermanent capital for impermanent goods, somehow, there lingered a graceful, spirited, permanence, too. Maybe that is what made the wizard so happy.

When Chris was 6 we went to buy birthday candles and a fishing pole. Chris also saw some candy. I turned to pick up the NY Times, and saw Chris reach up to the counter with his purchase. The wizard stood gleaming and ready. Then Chris took out his wallet and stared up. He fished in the little pouch, and found his coin. Then the wizard looked at Chris, and Chris looked at the wizard. The old eyes darkened with delighted understanding, and the handlebar mustache twitched and the wrinkled hand reached forward. And Chris held his ground and waited, fingering the coin, for that eternal moment that hangs between childhood and maturity. There they stood, matador and bull, boxer and champion, batter and pitcher, wizard and boy. As he had for decades, the shop owner patiently paused. At last out came the coin. The deal was struck.

I count it as one of the holy moments I have seen, as is any first experience, and especially any first experience of impermanence. Sic transit gloria mundi.

The wizard died ten years ago. His son runs the place now, a sallow faced sullen, serious, saturnine, somber, sad soul. Gone are the mustache and panache of his father. Why is he so dour, I have wondered over the years? I think I know. The son is my age. *Young.* He remembers those holy moments too, those experiences of entering the world, those moments when we learn about impermanence, those early exchanges over goods that are seasonal as, in fact, are all goods in this world. He remembers his dad reaching down to take the coin, to seal the deal, to shake with happiness in the sunlight streaming over all the little impermanence of life. And it makes him sad. He misses his dad. He misses his dad. And don't we all? And don't we all.

Once we begin to reckon with the impermanence of this life, so much paper and candy and seasonal needs, there comes a longing for an experience of God. There arises in the heart, a longing for an experience of God, for the lapping light of the morning to touch the cheek, for the full permanence of . . . *grace, love, heaven* . . . to enter our boyish life.

People come to church for an experience of God. You would be surprised to know how hard, even in the ministry, it can be to keep his truth in view. Men and women come to church, longing for an experience of divine love.

The son, the new shopkeeper, needs a church, a place where the longing of the heart can be fed, that *"desire of the moth for the flame, of the night for the morrow, the devotion to something afar from the sphere of our sorrow."*[1] And don't we all? And don't we all.

A PROPHETIC APPROACH TO IMPERMANENCE

The same longing we have tried to witness in the crowded aisles of the village green five and dime also pulses through the deep places of the Scripture. Blessed are those who hunger and thirst. Micah Ben Imlah did hunger and thirst, too. In the pain and tenderness of too much loving, he wondered how, if at all, such an experience could be his. *With what shall I come before the Lord? What shall I do? Whom should I love? How should I walk?*

Amid the piles and aisles of impermanent, seasonal goods, where an experience of lasting love?

A path toward the permanent, this is what Micah desires. In the uses of his resources, Micah believes, there lies hidden the potential for an opening into an experience of God. Underneath that apparently chaotic impermanence, there lies the potential for an opening into the experience of God. Micah advises us not to get too comfortable.

Do. We may learn to use our resources for the making of justice.

Love. We may come to love what cannot be seen, mercy, and then to use what can be seen, money, rather than loving what can be seen and using what cannot be seen.

Walk. Because our transactions, most days, involve bills and not coins, we, unlike the shopkeeper, we are more tempted to take ourselves overly seriously.

---

1. Shelly.

PAUL AND IMPERMANENCE

In this same vein, the Apostle to the Gentiles teaches us again today about impermanence. Is this not a glorious and a liberating word? In treating a matter of moral discernment among the wayward Corinthians, Paul asserts the impermanence of this world. His blessed words are as strange for us as they are healthy to hear.

Paul advises us not to get too comfortable. Marriage, death, birth, work, life, all—these Paul asserts are themselves impermanent goods, seasonal items in the aisles of life's five and dime. Good, holy, important, and, at last . . . impermanent. Let those who buy do so as those who have no goods. Let them recall that first experience, reaching up to the counter, of impermanence. Let us treat our goods not in the form of this world, which is passing away, but in the form of the world to come.

Here is a great blessing, for those with ears to hear. Within the land of impermanence, there is the possibility of an experience of God. It is for that experience . . . that touch of the divine hand upon the hand of the child of God . . . for which goods and seasonal items and crowded aisles and everything from five and dimes to great corporations exist.

When we give, we open the possibility of experiences of God, not necessarily for ourselves directly, although that may be, but more often indirectly for others. Giving and generosity bless us because they open up the opportunity for an experience of God.

IMPERMANENCE TODAY

As stewardship Sunday approached this year, I began to pray about what to say.

Free Will Offering

I wanted to say something about the power and beauty of our free will system of giving and funding. You are free to give or not, to tithe or not. It is a rare and divine grace. So . . .

There is an anxiety about this day. This is my 23rd stewardship sermon, fall campaign and annual financial plan. Every one is an adventurous ride on the tide of generosity. We have no tax base in the church, like those which support schools. We have no product to barter, like those that support businesses. We live and die on the free choices, every fall, that raise a tide of giving. I wonder, sometimes, what would happen if we could not fund our ministry? What would happen to our efforts with children and older folks, our mission and outreach, our staff and buildings, our worship and music? Yet every year, we await the news of the tide.

In 1995, I was heading into another role, a district superintendency. I confess that one apparent minor happiness about that assignment was the prospect that there would be no pressure to raise funds every fall. I would just send out the note assigning the 20% to each church for apportionment, and wait for the checks to role in. A little ice tea, Oprah on the tube, wait for the mail to come. No need to worry. No attention to freedom for the giver. No anxiety about the amount.

You notice I didn't last very long as a DS. David Lubba said, "Come to Asbury and enjoy a great pulpit, a fine building, beautiful music, super staff, loving congregation, full mission. And, after five years, you can buy a slightly used new car." Yes, I said in a New York minute. Later I asked, "What about stewardship?" Yes, there is that...

Every fall the church waits for the tide, like surfers. We crouch along the board, out beyond the San Francisco Bay. The sun is high, the sky is blue, the air is warm, the day is fine. We feel the tide rising, and here it comes! We stand, and put our toes out on the board. We hang ten. And the tide rises, every year. Thanks to freely chosen gifts, thanks to you. Sometimes the tide is low, and we drift a little. Sometimes the tide is high, and we spin. The uncertainty that is the sign of real freedom for the giver and the gift is that warm and vivifying wind that feeds us. I wanted to talk to you about freedom in giving.

Developing Disciples

But then I realized it was not just free giving I wanted to address.

I wanted to celebrate the ministry of this church, its worship and education and care. This great church does so much good in the world! Here children learn of Christ, receiving Bibles from an adult class. Here the hungry are fed, and given a haircut. Here the worship of God resounds in high praise, as our radio congregation listens in. Here our mature members put young adults to shame with spiritual retreats that are real occasions of spirit. Here grown men pray at 6 A.M. Some of us are still groaning at noon. Here our frail elderly are not forgotten, but visited with a word of hope and prayer by a retired minister. Here fellowship and friendship can grow into adult classes. Here the Scripture is read and interpreted from a sturdy pulpit. Here Philippians 4:8 shines, things that are *honorable, true, just, beautiful, of good report*. There is a story a day to tell about Jesus Christ who inhabits, haunts and hallows this church! I wanted to talk with you about the ministry of AFUMC.

Faithful Saints

But then I saw that the ministry of the church alone was the heart of the matter either.

I wanted to tell about the faithful people here, who year in and year out generously, happily support the work of Christ here. One is an elderly man, gracious and loving, who learned at an early age to tithe. One is a fiercely able Trustee, who cares for the property and investments of the church, but who has a big heart for the poor in Honduras. One is a woman who has prayed mission into life, and has had the grace to live with surprising answers to prayer, answers other than what she expected. This is real stewardship! I wanted to tell the stories of holy people here today. How would I limit the list to fit the twenty-two minute sermon?

An Experience of God

But then I sensed that something more than this too was in my heart.

I wanted to speak to what you look for at church, an experience of God. People come to church for an experience of God. It is great blessing, that giving opens opportunities for experiences of God. They come in God's time and they come over time and they come to others. But giving gives the chance for such an experience.

A month ago I had a wedding here in the chancel. It was beautiful autumn day as so many have been this year. The service was wonderful. Duane played a version of "Love Divine" with bells that rounded off the service to perfection. I was proud to be here. Later, in the ready room, a woman who had attended the service asked about my family.

We talked, and I discovered that she was from the North Country, and had been raised with some difficulty by a single mother.

"Near Alexandria Bay?"

"In Alexandria Bay."

"Did you know Rev. Pennock, who was there in retirement?" (who is Jan's grandfather)?

All of sudden her face became red and her eyes filled. I wondered what I had said to upset her. This is the "joy" of the ministry—you enter a room and everyone is uncomfortable! You make small talk and women cry!

"No", she said, "you don't understand . . . When I was a young woman, I barely could go to college. Every semester I received a check from the Alexandria Bay Church, money that was to pay for my voice lessons… This kept me going in college, not just the money, which was significant, but more so the thought, the fact that somebody believed in me, could see me with a future, outside of my struggling family and small town, and invested in me . . ."

By now we were both emotional.

What does that have to do with me?

"I learned a few years ago that your wife's grandfather is the one who gave the money for those lessons! His gift formed my life!

What are you doing today?

"I am the Director of Music for a Methodist church near Albany. The bride grew up in my youth choir. Music is my life."

Over all those years, and so many miles, across such a great existential distance, look what happened: I was given an experience of God, emotion laded and heartfelt and real and good, and even in church or at least almost, as a consequence of a gift made long ago and far away. The hidden blessing of generosity is that giving opens the world to the possibility of experiences of God. Rev. Harold Pennock is long dead. His wife Anstress is long dead. But here, after a wedding, in the late afternoon, his thoughtful kindness opened the world. I wanted to commend to you an experience of God.

Why Am I Here?

But then I realized there was even something more I wanted to say, more than the goodness of AFUMC, more than faithfulness of her people, more than the experience of God provided in generosity.

I wanted to speak, and that very personally, of the reason I am here.

What is lasting and good in my life has come from the church of Christ. Name and identity in baptism. Faith in confirmation. Community in eucharist. Wife and family in marriage. Work, and vocation, in ordination. Saving forgiveness in moments of pardon. Hope for heaven in the gospel of Christ.

Whatsoever has any permanence for me comes from the church.

So . . . I guess I would be lost in the fall without a chance to preach a Stewardship sermon. (I admit it has been twenty-three years since I have had the chance to be so lost! . . . but nevertheless.)

But I am here, really, out of a formation, long before adulthood, in the midst of people who knew that the form of this world was passing away. The superintendents who remembered to bring Christmas gifts, the Bishops who sat at the dining room table - they did so with an existential reserve, a freedom from the impermanence of this world, a joyful and sober sense that the form of this world is passing away. "Don't get too comfortable" they seemed to say in deed as well as word. They modeled an existential itinerancy that is far more important the mechanical one we know too well in which, as we say, Bishops appoint—and disappoint. The ministers who came and sang hymns in our homes, who laughed at and with each other, and who prayed for the salvation of the world—they dealt with the world as if they had no dealings with it. The people in our churches, churches supported then and now by the tithing of retired school teachers, who cared about the world and about the next generation—they knew the impermanence of the world around, and the brevity of our time here. They tithed, and so what remains of our church remains.

Those who raised us, who could have had many more the goods of this passing world, lived with an aplomb, a grace, a savoir faire that better than any sermon interpreted 1 Corinthians 7. Let those who mourn do so as if they were not mourning. The discipline of the Methodists—this is your birthright—comes from this presentiment about impermanence.

In our raising, you could have the courage to live on less, to itinerate at the direction, if not the whim, of a Bishop, to pull up stakes and make new friends, to know the hurt and the excitement of a gypsie life. How did they do this? Because they believed in their bones that what lasts is not the various goods and seasonal items of the five and dime, but the touch of the wizard's hand. That gracious experience of God that comes in and through the impermanent cacaphony of life, and is primed by giving.

I wonder if we are ready to open the world up to experiences of God?

A MIDNIGHT PRAYER

Sometime later tonight, especially if the sky is clear and if the stars come out, I am going to walk out onto the back lawn. The moonlight glistening on the frosted hedgerows, the sound of squirrels scurrying with nuts to store, the smell of the dampened leaves, the taste of crisp autumn—the season of accountability—touching the tongue, hands clasped against the cold now beneath a gleaming North Star it is time to offer a prayer. I wonder if you would pray this with me tonight:

Dear God,

Help me to love you this coming year.

I am going to give away 10% of what I earn. I am nervous about doing it. I need your help. I want to tithe, but the coin seems to stick inside the wallet somehow. So I need your help. Amen.

7

"A Promise Before Dark"

Amos 9:11–15; 1 Corinthians 15:42–55

STREETLIGHTS

I MEET YOU THIS morning, wandering along the meadow of the heart, walking closely in the village green of the soul. We must clearly identify, this morning, where we stand. I stand with you, speaking out of hope, standing in hope, dressed in hope. The preacher, apparently isolated behind a pulpit and robed in centuries of tradition, can stand in many places: in fear, in longing, in hunger, in happiness, in doubt. It is important today that we identify our meeting place. I am speaking out of a great hope today.

Sunday lets us pause and kick through the park leaves under foot. In the tolling of the Baptist bells, we hear the promise of words that have meaning (9/10). In the space of the green, we see the promise of God's capacious grace (9/17). In the little library to the left, we thumb through the promise of justice (9/24). In the depression era post office to the right, we read the promise of truth (10/15). In the humble Methodist church, we leaf through the altar Bible, with its promises of love and freedom (10/22). In Jesus Christ it is always Yes! All the promises of God find their Yes in Him!

Now the night is falling on our simple English commons, our Yankee green. The day is far spent and night is at hand. You remember that we have been told to come home before dark. This is the rule in our town, that at the end of the day, we go home. We tarry here, along the soul's village green, the green pastures of salvation, where the soul is restored, we tarry that is for a time, but we all are going home, come nightfall. We are free to love, and how we love freedom, but at last the twilight falls. On some hidden cue, right at dusk, all of the streetlights along the green are illumined. Six hours shalt thou play, but the seventh is a Sabbath unto the home, and thou shalt go home, when thou dost see the streetlights come on.

Is there a lasting promise that we may take with us, a promise before dark, that we may hold in our hearts as the leaves rustle underfoot, and as the streetlights brighten, and as we turn the last corner home? And is not our response to this one question, perhaps, the single most profound response we can give to anything or anyone? Have we hope for the future, hope for heaven, hope for life today?

A NEW CREATION (APOCALYPSE): AMOS AMENDED

A few weeks ago I went for three days to Dallas for an annual meeting. We stayed in the Fort Worth Texas Radisson. It happens that this is the hotel that President and Mrs. Kennedy stayed in the last night of his life, November 21–22, 1963. Our host pastor, had been at the same hotel early that morning. His dad took him to shake the President's hand as they left for that fateful automobile ride. Because they arrived at 6 A. M. and stood along the rope for hours, his was one of the hands touched. That night Kennedy gave his last speech. There are pictures on the wall from that evening, Jack and Jackie and others.

One of the ministers said, looking back to this date, and his own life at age nineteen when the news came: "I remember the deep anguish and pain I felt over this tragic loss. It was probably the first time I began to ask God "Why? Why do such tragedies happen in this world? Why do promising Presidents get assassinated? Why do children die of cancer?" Perhaps that event was such a quickening event for you too.

The prophet Amos asserted that for Israel, too, the day would arrive when the chickens would come home to roost. His prophecy proved as accurate as it was chilling. In fact, the prophecy of Amos ends without any word of redemption at all: "I will set my eyes upon them for evil and not for good."[1] But when the Bible was assembled, and this could have been during the time of the Babylonian captivity, a later writer added the words we heard this morning: "The days are coming . . . when the mountains shall drip sweet wine and the hills shall flow with it . . . I shall restore the fortunes of my people . . ." [2]

This is the kind of promise that Israel associated with the Messiah. It comes from the time that the prophetic hope was modulating into apocalyptic expectation, a time much later than that of Amos himself. From this time, as Christian people, we continue to inherit a sense of hope and expectation that one day, one fine day, the earth will be full of the glory of God as the water covers the sea. Like Moses, we may not see it in our lifetime. Like Amos, we may not even print such an expectation in our personal prophecies. Like Jesus, we may look in vain for the fulfillment of this hope, this expectation, in our own time. Still, he has taught us to pray: "Thy kingdom come on earth."[3] It is that prayer that lies at the heart of the appendix to Amos, read earlier. Thy kingdom come, for nations who lose promising leaders. They kingdom come, for families torn apart and put back together. Thy kingdom come, for communities uneasy about an uncertain economy. Thy kingdom come, for those hungering and thirsting and lonely and lost. Thy kingdom come, on earth, as already it is in heaven.

There is a horizon of hope that opens out in the voices of the prophets, that is not silenced but only amplified by the Gospel of Jesus Christ. These promises, for the earth we know, seem so unlikely, so distant, so frail. Yet here they are. The lion will lie down with the lamb. They shall not hurt or destroy in all my holy mountain. God will wipe away every tear from their eye.

For all our stumbling here in the foothills of life, we dare not ignore the great peaks of expectation, which more than we know give us our identity.

Heaven is out there, coming toward us from the completion of history.

So, with Paul Tillich we can have the courage to be, and with John Kennedy we can find profiles in courage, and with Parker Palmer we can

---

1. Amos 9:4.
2. Amos 9:13–14.
3. Matthew 6:10.

muster the courage to teach, and with Albert Camus we can develop the courage to travel.

A RESURRECTION BODY (GNOSIS): PAUL ATTENDED

As G. Bernanos reminds us, the greatest sin is the denial of hope. While it is true that where there is life, there is hope, it is truer still that where there is hope there is life. Today we receive a word of hope, and a look to the future. Hope that is seen is not hope. Who hopes for what he sees? But if we hope for what we do not see, we wait for it with patience.

As Paul completes his letter to the wayward Corinthians, he offers us again his account of resurrection, the resurrection, precisely, of the dead. We notice that Paul minces no words as he acknowledges our death. We perish. That perishing, as Madame Bovary discovered, can be difficult, even ignoble. We lose a physical body, or are planted as physical bodies. We are dust, and to dust we return. Says Paul: flesh and blood cannot inherit the kingdom of God.

For Paul, as for the earliest church in general, this great hope was expressed in the religious garb of his day, the language and imagery of apocalyptic.

If for this life only we have hoped in Christ, we are of all people most to be pitied.

Hardly a single week passes in this church without the report that someone has "fallen asleep." Every such communication carries a weight, often as unbearable as it is unspeakable of grief. In the midst of life we are in death. As Paul said of himself, "We are perishing every hour."[4]

Here blunt and terse, realistic and brief, the gospel summons is heard—A mystery, after all—is all we take with us before dark. Either we hold this promise, or we have nothing whatsoever at all. All the promises of God concludes in this Promise Before Dark. Love outlasts death. Earthly struggle bears a lasting heavenly meaning. Patent tragedy and injustice are part of a larger, longer, latent, loving story. Sin does not have the last word. So it is with the resurrection of the dead.

All that I have seen and known has given me ample cause to trust God for all I cannot see and do not know. Who are we to question God's resurrection it is rather the resurrection that questions us. This is our hope.

---

4. 1 Corinthians 15:30.

A CURRENT REALITY (PRESENCE): CHURCH

The promise of Christ also rests upon us in this present life and nourishes us with a glorious hope, long before the mountains drip with wine, and well apart from the mystery of resurrection and imperishability and immortality. Amos's uninvited editor looked out toward a day of heavenly earth. Toward this same far-off horizon we also walk. Paul's rhapsodic resurrection poem looks up toward a place of earthly heaven. Beneath it's same apocalyptic longing we also live. How thrilling our common life could become if we were perpetually infused with such hope, if every step trod toward heaven on earth and every breath awaited a location in Heaven! As those baptized in Christ, we have the least to fear and the most to desire. In Baptism we have already died. So we walk in newness of life, looking out and looking up. The mountains will drip with wine. One day. What is perishable will become imperishable, one day. Especially on those dark paths in history and especially as night falls for every one of us, such a hope shall guide us.

The confidence of Christ in his people testifies in the affirmative. There is a present hope of the Holy Spirit that lives just as truly as the future hope for the creation and the higher longing for redemption, the resurrection of the body. St. John (to him finally we must turn) said, "This is eternal life: to know Jesus Christ." Look out and look up, but look here too! Every so often, we have a radiant glimpse of the completion of time and space. Every worship hour can become such a radiant glimpse, as can a fellowship meeting, a word of service, a spiritual retreat, a joyful birthday, an hour of deliberation. Enough hours come along to keep us going.

But what about today? What about the ordinary, less than glorious, simple hours of yesterday and today and tomorrow? Is there "Heaven in a grain of sand and Heaven in a wild flower?"

A FRIEND'S STORY

Emory Purcell writes, "*When I was a child, there were often missionaries or evangelists staying with us. One I remember most fondly was Mary Schlosser. About fifty years of age then, she had been a missionary in China for many years.*

All of us have heard stories of how missionaries forced native people to give up their culture and become westerners; how missionaries were tools of capitalistic colonialism. Some were indeed. But not Mary Schlosser. All she talked about were, not her converts, but the boys and girls in her school in China: how bright and eager and loving they were. She had high hopes for each of them and had arranged for some of them to go abroad to prestigious universities to study. She knew that one day they were going to make significant contributions to their people.

Now, you never read about Mary Schlosser in Time. As a young woman she had had a promising career ahead of her. The call to China persuaded her to pour out her life there. After I knew her, Mary Schlosser spent many years in a communist prison camp in China and died shortly after her release.

I did read about Mary Schlosser a few years ago. A group of dissident students from China had been interviewed by a religious news editor. They talked about the missionaries who had taught their parents at a school in Kaifung. Among the names remembered were Clara Leffingwell and Mary Schlosser.

I have a sense that Mary Schlosser's resurrected life is only beginning. It is love, finally, that surpasses money and power; and overcomes tragedy. Mary Schlosser poured out her life in love for her boys and girls. Through her love, broken as it was, God's love poured through more and more to life down through the generations.

The thing I remember about Mary Schlosser is her radiance. Was she happy? I don't know. It is, in fact, an irrelevant question. Mary was radiant. In her enthusiasm and in the greatness of her soul, the sun shown on us. This is our hope.

Rudyard Kipling was once addressing students at McGill University in Montreal. The lure of having things and even the power of success all sound so good if you listen quick. Yet, powerful successful egotism is the ultimate failure. Kipling said:

Someday, you will meet a person who cares for none of these things. Then you will know how poor you are.

Over the years I have been privileged to know many people who are rich the way Mary Schosser was rich. Sunday school and public school teachers - parents and young people - bosses and workers. People who have poured out their lives in love so that God's love can bring life.

I want to suggest that is what has actually made America great: not all the things we have to be happy; but, rather, the generous people who pick *up the cross of human need-people whose radiant lives testify to life beyond the cross.*"[5]

DARK AND DEEP

Let us look out to the future, trusting the promise of hope.
    Let us look up to the resurrection, trusting the promise of hope.
    Let us look here and, trusting the promise of hope.

---

5. Emery Purcell, private correspondance.

Homiletical Appendix

STUDENTS OF SCRIPTURE AND preaching from Lemoyne College, McGill University, Colgate Rochester Divinity School, Northeastern Seminary, and United Seminary at Buffalo have helped in various ways to develop the material collected here. Here and there, some will recognize the crystallization of classroom debate in sermonic illustration, while others will notice places where the teacher learned the lessons provided by student experience. A word of thanks goes these men and women who, over the last ten years, have had the courage to search the Scripture and there to seek meaning for today.

Their successors may be encouraged (or required!) to read these pages, as preparation for biblical study or for preaching from the prophets and Paul. For these future, as yet unforeseen colleagues in study, a little list of homiletical devices here illustrated is appended. The list follows the exhaustive but ultimately unequaled presentation in D. Buttrick, *Homiletic: Moves and Structures* (1988). (The notations refer to sermon (i.e. I) and section (i.e. 4)).

More generally, one could inspect here a variety of sermonic issues: the blessing and curse of the extended metaphor; the use of spatial, temporal, logical, and irenic designs; the wisdom of five moments/points/moves in today's sermon; the durability and limitations of Yankee English; use of sustained conversation and dialogue; the place of poetry; the advisability of litanies and repetition as formal devices; the opportunities that lie beyond mere lectionary and mere narrative preaching.

TOOLS IN THE PREACHER'S WORKSHOP[1]

VI, 1/3/4	1. Structural modes: a. Immediacy (VI, 1); b. Reflection (VI, 3); c. Praxis (VI, 4).
II, III, V	2. Hermeneutical Proposals: a. Community (II); b. Duality (III); c. Symbolism (V)
IV, 3	3. Moves/Points: a. Theological Understanding; b. Opposition; c. Real Experience (IV, 3).
I, 1/2/3	4. Points/Warning: a. Point of View (I,1); b. Transition (I,1); c. Start/Stop (I, 3).
VII, 5/3/2	5. Images: a. Analogy; b. Denial; c. Interpretation.
II, 1/2/4/5	6. Style: a. Concrete (II,1); b. Adjective (II,2); c. Pronouns (II,4); d. Present Active (II,5).
III, 1/2/3/4	7. Rhetorical Forms: a. Bringing Out (III, 1); b. Associating (III,2/3); c. Disassociating (III,4)
I,1; II, 4/5; V, 3	8. Rhetorical Orientations: a. Spatial (I,1); b. Temporal (II, 5); c. Personal (V,3); d. Social (II, 4).

---

1. Buttrick, Homiletic, 1988.

Part 2

Once More to the Lake

8

Health

Mark 7:24-37

TO THE LAKE

HALF OF THE GOSPEL happens Upstate! Jesus meets us this fall along the lakeshore, in the north country, by the Sea of Galilee. Are we holding up our end of the stick? Have we balanced the teeter-totter as promised? Are we alive to His Presence in Our Place? The first half of Mark's Gospel, and thus all subsequent Gospels, happen Upstate.

The Sea of Galilee, to the north, resembles nothing so much as one of our own Finger Lakes. If you stand in Capernaum, at that Lake's northern tip, and look due south, you see for ten miles an inland fresh lake, about 2 miles wide, resting in the sloping embrace of hillsides like our own here in Upstate New York. Jerusalem, the great city, is found due south. People go to Jerusalem from the north. Especially for festivals, as we go to the great city on the Island of Manhattan. Go south for Sukkoth or Macy's Thanksgiving Party. Go south for Hanukah or the New Year's lights. Go south for Passover or the Easter Parade. New York City is to Jerusalem as the Finger Lakes are to Galilee. Downstate, Upstate. Northern Kingdom, Southern Kingdom. Both have their place. But come to lakeshore for lessons about living.

I was encouraged in July by a good old friend to drive with him along the western shore of Cayuga Lake. It is a road from memory and youth, one on which I had not driven in 20 years. Ladies and Gentlemen of the jury, I ask you, is there really a more beautiful summer sight than Lake Cayuga from its crest along route 89 south? Slow down for cyclists. Pass by the Blue Heron. Catch a glimpse of Taughannock Bask, Bathe, Breathe in the pure health of deep greens and blues on a sun spangled jewel of a lake! We came near the hospital in Ithaca, a place of wondrous change, the house in which our two older children and so many others were born. Bernice Danks taught generations of nurses there, using particularly her favorite epigram: "we call things routine because they are the most important things we do." Lay Leader, lead soprano, member to conference, Veterinarian's wife, head of nursing instruction, Bernice embodied today's gospel. As we come once more to the Lake today, the Gospel is health! Jesus heals. We know how to heal. Your health matters.

We Remember Jesus Who Heals

In the first place, let us firmly hold the centuries old memory that Jesus was a divine healer. Along the shores of the Sea of Galilee, upon paths perhaps familiar to him from youth, Jesus (always here in Mark's particular memory) preached and taught and healed. Jesus did more healing than anything else: by the time we reach Mark 7:24 Jesus has already banished an unclean spirit, cured Peter's mother in law, cast out and silenced demons, cleansed a leper, stood up a paralytic, repaired a withered hand, exorcised the Gerasene demoniac whose name is Legion, brought Jairus' daughter back from the brink of death, staunched by a touch a flow of blood, made alive the synagogue ruler's daughter, "and as many as even touched his garment were made well." Those who are well have no need of a physician, but those who are sick do. The healthy beauty that is our home here Upstate lies at the heart of the Christian Gospel.

I worked for a man once who spent a third of his adult life in Switzerland, but he hated cheese and never wore a watch. You have heard of people who reside in our sister city, Buffalo, but have never seen Niagara Falls. I expect there are people who live in Rochester who have no interest in photography, and not the slightest appreciation for photocopies. We can name two people who live in Syracuse but have not ever shopped at the Mall. (I am one of them). One man who lives in San Diego doesn't own sunglasses and has never surfed and wouldn't recognize a Beach Boys song. Are there Alaskans who despise igloos? Lord have mercy. Frenchmen who dislike wine? Saints preserve us. Hawaiians who won't swim? Oh, pshah. Methodists who can't sing? Heavenly day. What an earthly shame, all. I hope someone is shutting the windows of heaven whenever there arises such bald lack of appreciation for what has been given! Sin is refusing to receive what we are given.

God's natural bounteous gift to Upstate is the Finger Lakes, a world-class handful of beauty. It is natural setting for healing, for healthy living. In the Gospel of Mark, at every turn, Jesus meets us with healing. Before we begin too quickly to debate the theological nuances of the healing ministry recorded in Mark, may we look at the big picture? Let's stand for a moment on the lakeshore and take in the whole beautiful body of water. However finally you understand the Gospel record, there is no mistaking the sharp thrust, the surgical cut, the saving remedy of today's Gospel. Jesus is mightily concerned with health, with healing. Whatever else the earliest Christians remembered of his lakeside ministry, his upstate work, this much is sure: Jesus is mortally concerned with healing.

The lessons of Tyre and Sidon, here along the Sea of Galilee, are lessons in living that sharply engage Jesus in the hard work of healing. In fact, Jesus continues toward healing even across two prodigious boundaries. Here is what I mean.

The concern of second Temple Judaism for cleanliness included a significant wariness about interaction with non-Jews. There is no mistaking the abiding influence of these kosher codes in the text that may be Jesus' harshest comment: "we don't feed dogs."[1] If any dominical saying is historical this surely must be for it is so uncomplimentary, so unflattering. Every editor to Mark and beyond would have ample reason to erase it. We might have done it ourselves. Jesus is a person of his time: speaking Aramaic, thinking David wrote the Psalms, riding donkeys, wearing sandals, expecting the Apocalypse, picturing a flat world, and, yes, concerned about the cleanliness codes: "it is not fair to feed the children's food to dogs." But hold the good news! Remember Jesus the Healer! At this, the only point in Mark's gospel that it occurs, Jesus stretches out beyond Judaism, beyond inherited religion, beyond cult and culture, beyond tradition. There is something more important to him. Health.

---

1. Matthew 7:24–30.

Here is a mother who craves her daughter's health. Jesus hears her voice, honors her need, heals her daughter. Health takes Him beyond the barrier of religion.

There is no mistaking the power of this pronouncement for the 70ad church in Rome, make up of Gentiles. They, we, all are included in the healing ministry of Jesus.

There is a still more personal barrier that Jesus also crosses today. As so often in the Gospel of Mark, Jesus hides. Have you ever noticed that? Read Mark again this afternoon, and it will jump off the page at you. A dozen times at crucial moments, Jesus hides. He heals a woman, then says "shh." He gathers a crowd, then says "shoo." He preaches with magnificence, then "strictly charges them to tell no one." He tries, according to Mark, to keep his nature a secret. No one really has fully explained the Messianic Secret of Mark. We need not try this morning. What is astounding, however, is that Jesus will not let this personal barrier—his hiding—keep him from healing. There is something more important to him than his own safety. Health. A man begs, and Jesus heals.

Health is more valuable than religion and more precious than safety. Jesus heals. Says Mark.

We Know How to Heal

In the second place, we too know something about healing. People need more reminders than insights. Truth, saving truth, comes often in the guise of a forgotten understanding. Our friends, our church, our families, at their best, give us ourselves by reminding us of Truth we used to know well.

I understand that we have some ongoing struggles in health care around our fair city. I read about it in the paper. I hear about it on the phone. I learn about it in conversation. The Christian Gospel, though, is an empowering reminder to those sturdy souls, many present today, who are laboring in the corporate work of healing. It takes a community to heal a body. Real healing is holy, in the sense that whatever is holy is at least whole: real healing attends to the whole human being: body, mind, spirit, community. We know about this. Here.

We know how to heal. We know about healing, or at least we used to know. I have clipping in my sermon box from a newspaper article in September of 1992. There is a heated political debate flooding the Presidential election. Disagreement and dissent abound. There were more points of view on healthcare then, than there are gubernatorial candidates in California today. But there is consensus, says this article, about one thing. There is at least one city in the country that knows how to do things right. There is at least one community, and this in the area of the Seas of Galilee—the Finger Lakes—that is a model for what might be. There is a point of promise, what one calls a part of the new covenant and the other calls simply a point of light. It is as if the whole country is seated around the TV together, watching the World Series. There is no agreement about anything, until, sitting on his haunches, Uncle Bill or was it Uncle George, says: "well, it can be done. I mean look at the way they do things in Rochester." And all 260 million eat another potato chip and nod their heads in agreement.

I have no interest in going backward. Generally. Once though Jan and I were driving somewhere and, remarkably, we got lost. I know it is impossible to imagine. At some point it was suggested: "maybe we should turn around and go to where we knew where we were going."

In short, I hope this year to read two books, both as yet unwritten. You may write one, or both: one on what has happened to us in the last decade; one on what we can do in the next. Take heart. The day is coming when across this land, men and women will point to our city and say: "health—they know about that in Rochester!"

What is true of medicine is true of ministry. Spiritual health is a communal endeavor. We have come to a time to build in our ministry! To build space, relationships, habits of welcome, an open vibrant spiritual village green to focus all that is lastingly good across our county. Your church leadership is preparing to get some fresh air in here, to let a clean wind blow through a new century of ministry, to open up space and place for grace.

I wonder if a visitor here, today, hearing of our plans for a welcoming space, might particularly hear this morning's gospel. You are sitting perhaps in the back pews, with a child or two. You hear that this church is setting out to build space to welcome newcomers. It dawns on you that many of the people giving most of the effort to this will not necessarily benefit directly from it. They are giving to an unknown future, an unforeseen generation. They are giving of their resource for people they don't know, a generation yet unacquainted with Christ, a generous gift with no strings and no expectations. Given to you. You are being included! That is the feeling Mark's church had to hear about Jesus healing a Gentile, one of them. In ministry as well as medicine, we have known what makes for health. Look what others gave us, no strings, no mortgage. It is time for us to do our part.

Your Health Matters

In the third place, these two healing accounts force upon us a therapeutic way of viewing the world. Staying again simply with the main thrust of these ancient readings, it is scarcely possible to hear Mark 7:24 and discount your own health. Health mattered enough for Jesus to break the barriers of religion and safety. Health has thus been central to the church's ministry, and central to our city's history. Which means this: your health matters. I suppose I could dress it up a little bit and make the interpretation a little more theologically obscure: "your personal and physical well-being are valued in this dominical periscope that defines the Markan presentation of the Christ." Or, just, your health matters.

You were made in the image of health. You deserve health. You were created for health. You ought to have health. You need health. Your health matters.

The word salvation is a Latin root term, coming up from the noun "salvus", which means, yes, health.

You will not expect, I know, that any interpretation of this Gospel can finally answer all of our questions about illness. We surely understand that the roots of disease are transgenerational, multicultural, and finally mysterious to a vast degree. Our Scriptures from the ancient world both veil and reveal insights about health. We can be more than joyful that our medical science is not that of first century Palestine. There is no way to explain why illness befalls saints and good health sinners. There is no way to understand the times and seasons for such episodes. You might as well blow against the wind, or stand on the shore and command the tide to turn.

And finally, the Lakeside Healer is the one who embraces us when, as is finally true for all, merely physical healing ceases.

But our gospel today makes a simpler and earlier affirmation. Your health matters. To God. To Christ Jesus. To the Spirit of Love. To those around you. To the mission of the church. You are meant for health! So, as you have breath and power: seek it, desire it, prepare for it, look for it, work toward, invest in it, share it, respect it, love it! How?

Spiritual health depends upon worship and prayer.
Fiscal health depends upon industry, frugality and tithing.
Relational health depends upon discipline, listening and awareness.
Physical health depends upon diet an exercise.
Psychological health depends upon friendship and rest.
Communal health depends upon justice and peace.
Professional health depends upon communication.
Sexual health depends upon commitment and fidelity and openness.
Religious health depends upon humility and honesty.

I was truly touched this summer to read my former teacher Elaine Pagel's book *Beyond Belief*. Her reflections begin with the illness and then the death of her younger child. Midway through her review of the Second Century church, she makes a simple observation about those who came to Christ in this period. A great many, she notes, came because they were hurting, or ill. They heard in the preaching of the Gospel a healing word. And they responded quickly. Others, she also notes, came more gradually, not out of immediate need, but with a thirst for 'living water.' Yet both earnestly desired health.

A MOMENT TO CHOOSE

We have affirmed the healthy lake setting of our region. First, we have heard the Gospel of Jesus who heals. Second, we have recalled our healthy tradition of medicine and ministry. Third, we have accepted that God loves us and that our health matters. There will be, on the minds of many, perhaps on your own, a thought now of a decision to be made, a choice to be entertained. The choice will be as varied as the congregation of several hundred here. It will be a choice as simple as leaving tobacco, or alchohol, or other addiction. As routine as a physical exam, a check up, a procedure. As challenging as a selection of care givers, providers, settings. As complex as a review of technical alternatives. Or, as sobering as the readiness to face the end of choices and the acceptance of God's embrace that is Eternal Health itself. To this choice, now, in a moment of silence, I invite you today.

9

Height

Mark 8:27–38

TO THE LAKE

IN A FEW CHAPTERS Jesus will turn south to leave his native Galilee and its lovely long lake. His way to the cross will take him to the cross roads of a world city. The first half of his Gospel happens though along the lakeshore, upstate if you will. This fall the Jesus of Mark's 70ad Gospel teaches us to the north beside the Lake of Genessaret. By spirit and interpretation we are privileged to hear these crucial lessons for living along our own lakeshores in the Finger Lakes. The Bible, as you have come to discover, in the main is not about Palestine, Jerusalem and Rome. Nor is it about Peter, Paul and Mary. Nor is it about temples, sandals or camels. It is about you. The Bible is about your life. The eastern shore of Canandaigua Lake (the chosen spot) is becoming some of the most valuable real estate in the country. How much more valuable are these lakeshore lessons which teach us about really being alive! They are some of the most valuable pedagogical landscape per sentence in literature. The first half of Mark, which is the model for all subsequent gospels, transpires upstate. Let us go once more to the lake!

A couple of years ago, in later autumn, our venerable 50+ class took a spiritual retreat southeast of Canandaigua at Watson Homestead. In their convivial embrace of one another, visible again in the careful plans laid out for their class's worship, education and care this year, and in their convivial embrace of the scattered assortment of children from other churches in the region also in residence that week, I could see emerging a moveable village green. For two days I watched a couple dotting on a pastor's children from the southern tier. This too is Christ: a place spiritually to meet, spiritually to greet, spiritually to watch our children grow and our grandparent's season. Together.

On return, in no hurry for once, we drove an alternate route and came northwest through Naples, toward the southern tip of Canandaigua, and into the Bristol "mountains." It is Thomas, the twin, who exclaims in late John: "My Lord and my God." His interest in seeing wonder murmured to us that day. How long has it been since you drove down an autumn day under the majestic cliffs in Naples. One of yesterday's cyclists said, "It looks like Switzerland." This glacially cut height! Height!

Yes, you may take the cable car from Gornergratt up the Matterhorn. That is height. You may drive up the dirt road from the Springs to Pike's Peak (passing Lutheran Ralph Anderson's new retirement home). That is height. You may climb Mt Marcy in the Adirondacks or Slide Mt in the Catskills. That is height. You may look out from the brown edge of the Grand Canyon. That too is height. But there is lake country height in Naples that bedazzles and bests them all. It is height with color. It is height with deep greens and blues. In the autumn with the large box of crayon colors! Height with grape pie for sale. Height at home. FDR pushed his wheel chair back from the canyon edge, puffing a cigar and offering that buoyant optimism which is the one quintessence of high leadership, to say: "This is nice, but take me home to upstate New York, to the green heights of my home. I like to see things grow."

As we come today to the lake, the gospel in a word is height. We are addressed at one of the high peaks of the Gospel. Looking out from a cave in Galilee, near the lake, Peter—and Mark's church in Rome in 70 and our church in Rochester in 2003—is stunned at last to see the Height of Christ!

The High Prize of the Upward Call of Christ

In the first place, our Gospel fixes Jesus' place at the height of life. This is a stylized passage, honed in the preaching of 40 years from Jesus to Mark, from Calvary to Rome. Peter is dead. Paul is dead. A third generation of faith is born. The small church in Rome (are there 50 souls?) faces daily danger. Some danger comes from persecution. More, though, comes from amnesia. Hence the writing of the sixteen chapters. Can you not imagine the profound reluctance of a community built on verbal resurrection, the ecstatic experience of life changing truth spoken and heard, heard and lived, lived and shared, to trap on paper what can only be said or sung? Only the frightful prospect of communal forgetfulness was worse. Hence, the documents. "Tell me again what Peter said!" "Where was it by the lake that Peter finally confessed his faith?" "How did the great fisherman put it—'Thou art the Christ'?" "What does this mean for us amid Caesars, lions, catacombs, persecutions, coliseums and prisons?" (We add: what could it mean for us in Rochester, 2 millennia hence?")

When at last he sees, Peter sees the Christ. He realizes that this same Jesus who teaches and heals and loves is none other than the one of whom there is none other. He is the height. In this one sense Christ as King above our portal here at Asbury First teaches us well. Peter fumbles as he fumblingly tries to explain Messiah (Greek: Christ) to the Gentiles in Rome. Later, the church will settle on a very clear term to make unmistakable the height of him who commands loving allegiance, and the loving allegiance to him who so commands. Lord. But Peter initially grasps for the very highest term given him by language, culture and tradition: "Thou art the Christ, the Son of the Living God."[1] What if Christ had come not to Galilee but to The Black Sea or the Yangtze or Tibet or the Euphrates or the Finger Lakes? "Did those feet in ancient time . . . ?" Had Peter grown up elsewhere, he would perhaps have spoken otherwise. A full platonic Greek like John will say, in a few years, Logos, Word. A shinto might have said, "The Silence." A Confucian, "Wisdom." A Moslem, "Prophet." An Iroquois: "Spirit." All mean what Paul meant: the name that is above every other name.

Our deepest longing, our truest hope, our finest action, our highest desire: these meet, across the human race, in the Christ of many names how is height, along the lake.

---

1. Matthew 16:16.

Christ Inspires Height

In the second place, Peter marks on Mark's wall for all time, including our own, an inspiration to height. Mediocre means half-way up the mountain. Christ is at the top.

One August 19 we sat on Mt Tremblant, the height of the Canadian Laurentians and quietly read the paper. We were recovering from summer. I wonder if others read David Anderson's column in the Times Sports section from that day? The dateline was Rochester, for all the world to read. All then news fit to print included that day a word about height. Anderson reviewed the PGA. He applauded the host city and its course at Oak Hill. He celebrated that older style courses "defense of par." The pro's fought the rough and the rough won. Then he quoted Tiger Woods, who knows something about height, and who has some right to speak about what is best. Here is what Woods said: "That is the hardest and fairest course I have ever played." That is a measure of height. You can live in Rochester NY. You can work in Rochester NY. You can serve the Lord with gladness in Rochester NY, right along the Finger Lakes shores, upstate, and be the best. Anywhere. The highest point. Anywhere. If you were a school, you could provide the best language program. If your were a corporation, you could provide the truest ethics and culture. If you were a hospital, you could provide the cleanest environment. If you were a church you could provide the best welcoming space. If you were a family business, you could provide the optimal employee support. Galilee of the gentiles, the North Country, was the outback of a third rate, vassal state. On its lakeshores were delivered life's sublimest lessons.

If you were Asbury First, which you are, you could provide excellence at the height of traditional worship, in the breadth of varied education, in the depth of missional care. You could become the spiritual village green of this county, the spiritual meeting place at the height of all things good.

What will take for your institution to "defend par?" And what will it take for our church to "defend par?" What will it take for our dear church in worship and education and care to be the toughest and truest anywhere? Christ as height evokes height. "Forgetting what lies behind and straining forward to what lies ahead I press on for the goal of the upward call of God in Christ Jesus."

As the pinnacle of piety Christ is no stranger to and needs no defense from other mountain peaks: Buddha, Hiawatha, Mohammed, Moses, all: "in him shall true hearts everywhere their high communion find; his service is the golden chord close binding humankind."

Sometimes you find the most height in depth, and the resurrection in a cross.

You Are Meant for High Living

In the third place, you are meant for some forms of height.

Sometimes our God is too small. JB Phillips crafted a fine little essay on that theme, years ago. Sometimes we hide ourselves behind a false humility that is really an inverted pride.

Have we forgotten so quickly the caring inspiration of the poets? "It asks of us a certain height . . ."

Have we forgotten so quickly the hard won courage of the pioneers? "Your playing small aids no one . . ."

Have we forgotten so quickly the dedication of our predecessors? "Here lies one whose greatest gift was to have done the best of things at the worst of times and to have hoped them in the most calamitous."

Have we forgotten Jim Collins, just a while ago, calling us to "a culture of discipline and an ethic of entrepreneurship"?

Have I forgotten Bill Coffin singing at the end of his first Riverside sermon: "This little light of mine, I'm gonna let it shine . . .?"

While it is true that sometimes we ask too much of one another and of ourselves, it is also true sometimes that we ask too little. Mark 8:27 is about height and cost and sacrifice.

We are led in faith to the open and ever new frontiers of what is true, honorable, just, lovely, excellent, of good report. New occasions teach new duties, time makes ancient good uncouth, one must upward still and onward, who would keep abreast of truth. Those who live to the utmost for God's highest praise are fearless before change, before newness, before adventure, before truth. And such a willingness is a virtue, like all virtues, formed by habit. Aristotle, Aquinas and Wesley all emphasized: virtues are formed by habit, daily ritual, weekly routine, virtues are formed by habit, as the spirit is nourished by reading a Psalm a day.

The past precedes but does not prescribe the future. Biology precedes but does not prescribe destiny. Family of origin precedes but does not prescribe identity. Home, hearth, culture, cult, church, school, town—they precede but they do not prescribe vocation. May we hear this as a word of faith? The past does not determine the future. There is always the open possibility of healing for past hurt. There is always the open possibility of forgiveness for past wrong. There is always the open possibility of liberation from past entrapment. This is what we mean by Christ. Thou art the Christ! "If anyone is in Christ, he is a new creation, the old has passed away and the new has come."[2] In the lasting and large, this is truly what we mean by resurrection.

DECISION

Along the lakeshore our gospel today is height. Christ is the world's height. Christ inspires height. You are meant for high living. Faith is a divine gift, but it is also a human choice. How are you going to live, high or low?

This flat, fearful one dimensional world culture all around us aches for authenticity, howls for height, expires for lack of example! I ask you Christian people at Asbury First in Rochester NY in 2003: please, do not hide your light under a bushel of mediocrity! You have never any reason to apologize for keeping your minds and heart on the newness of God, whatsoever things are true, honorable, just, pure, lovely, excellent, worthy of praise! Faith is a divine gift. Faith is also a human choice, as Peter found, evoked at height and by height. How are you going to live, high or low?

---

2. 2 Corinthians 5:17.

10

Home

Mark 9:38–41

TO THE LAKE

Amid all the versions of our life pinned to us like unrequested name tags, day by day, it is heartening to pause in the Presence of Christ and the hearing of his word. Friends help us see ourselves in a truer light. Families help us see ourselves in a fuller light. Pastors help us see ourselves in a broader perspective. The gathered church does the same and more for each of us. Finally, though, it is Christ who powerfully casts away the false demons of our supposed identities, and places us, like a ripe apple in an autumn sun, in a better light. We feel, Sunday, that what is right and good and happy about us has come home to us or we to Him.

We are at home upstate, as Jesus was raised north of the big city. His teaching in the first half of the Gospel occurs along the lakeshore, to the North in Galilee of the Finger Lakes, Galilee of the country and the many nations, Galilee of natural beauty. You can take the boy out of the country but is harder to take the country out of the boy. It is in the pastoral setting of the lake country that Jesus teaches lessons for living. Lessons for dying come later, downtown. Half of the Gospel is an upstate Gospel! Here, along the brilliant shining big sea water, you are not far from the kingdom of heaven!

You will recall the old saw about a Kansan who traveled across country, in this mythical tale, and found golden telephones in various churches. In Seattle, Austin, Michigan, Chicago, Milwaukee, Saskatoon, and Portland he located these fine phones, which were adorned with the sign, "$10,000 a minute." Every preacher explained: "that is the cost of a personal long distance call to heaven." Then he came to Auburn, NY, in the middle Finger Lakes, and saw the same phone, with a different sign, "25 cents." "Why not $10,000?" he asked. The reply, "Son you're in the Finger Lakes now. This is God's country. It is a local call here."

Not to put too fine a point on it. But. I have redundant purpose for my redundant reference, this autumn, to our lake side home, upstate. Everything north of Yonkers is one great sacred, secret garden! Have we truly appreciated what we have been given? Jesus hallowed his upstate home with teachings for living. Can we sense his Presence here? "Did those feet in ancient time . . ." We spend so much ink and bile on rust around us that we miss the main gift of rest around us. We live in a great, grand, lake filled, forest covered, river beaded, mountain viewed, glacier cut, divine park. Let us tend our garden. Let us celebrate what God has given us: meteorology, geography, history, community, spirituality. We can lead a progressive life together up here in Galilee. We may care for toddler and geezer, woman and gay, Latino and Asian. We can mow and shovel. It is a gift to be simple. It may take an existential shift. From creation to recreation. From employment to enjoyment. From manufacture to manumission. From achievement to appreciation. From speaking to listening. From building to believing. From the empire state to the state of grace. Jesus leads us once more to the lake today.

Christ Brings Us Home

First. The Scripture today announces again for us the glad tidings that Jesus brings us home. What a feeling that can be to come home! Do you remember your first real homecoming? Stepping of the train in uniform. Debarking the ship at port. Swinging a duffle bag from the bus after the first semester. The open hearted love of Christ continuously calls us home to his way, truth and life.

In this passage, Jesus answers a question about who can come home with the disciples. For whom is the good news? We receive teaching we want to receive, and usually only when we truly ask for something. Most preaching and teaching is lost because the hearer has back turned and face set in another direction. It is useless to holler people home. People will only hear you when they are coming toward you. As the disciples do this morning. Something has happened that is new and unplanned. The Gospel has taken off without them and they are worried. Others—others—are doing powerful deeds of good. Like Jonah under the castor oil plant, the disciples are disappointed to discover the uncanny, novel, expansive nature of God's invasion. They had rules set and a plan and a way forward. Now something has happened that is not in the manual. Others have heard. *Others.* Notice that John is concerned that others are not following "us," the disciples, though they clearly take the name of Christ, and do good in His spirit. There is a danger to breadth and there is a danger to narrowness. Here Jesus spanks out a clear word of inclusion. One papyri adds: "He that is not against you is for you. He that is far off today will be close tomorrow."

Two Methodists, earnest and eager, met at dawn to kneel and pray: "Holy God before you we are nothing. Nothing are we before you. You are great and we are nothing." A Presbyterian came by, and knelt too. "Holy God, before you I am nothing, nothing." Said one Methodist to the other, "Bob, hey, will you get this, look who thinks he's nothing!" Religion carries an inevitable curse of exclusivism unless it is regularly nourished by expansive grace. There is a wideness in God's mercy. More than one denomination will have a room in heaven. It is unshakable bedrock history that Jesus brought home, welcomed those outside: the poor, foreigners, children, women, the unclean, the sick. He is the Christ of the Open Heart!

Memorize his proverb: "He who is not against us is for us."[1]

You will lose the Gospel trail if you dwell too long on small differences. The first 200 years of the church's life saw a wide, wild range of heterodox expression, able to include both Matthew and John, which lived and let live in non-essential things. The assumption in Mark 9:40 is one great fellowship of love throughout the whole wide earth. Neither East nor West, neither Jew nor Greek, slave nor free, male nor female. One.

It is in this light that the sad exposure of ongoing rhetorical racism in our fair county can best be seen. It is underneath saying that public utterances of the kind we have heard by radio have no place in our home.

---

1. Mark 9:40.

We have not fully forgotten F. Douglass, S. Truth, H. Tubman, G. Smith or the 600,000 who died to preserve the Union. We remember ML King carefully calling Indianapolis "up south." Another generation is coming along that needs to hear the Gospel of the open heart! One poll showed 60% of this county largely untroubled by the virulent racism on our airwaves. The demon of racism needs still those who will cast it out, in the name of Christ. That is a job for you, disciples, as parents, employers, citizens. It is not only for those heroic leaders who expand boundaries by their presence: Bill Johnson and Violet Fischer and others. This is your job too.

My job today is to repeat that cultural prejudice and theological narrowness have no root in the Gospel. Jesus includes. Wesley had it right: "if thine heart be as mine, give me thine hand." There is a lot of space on a spiritual village green. Matthew in fear reversed the saying ("he who is not for us is against us").[2] Luke in kindness whitewashed the disciples ("they did not follow you"). Mark honestly both names our penchant for exclusivity, and reliably records Jesus word. Remember it this fall: "he who is not against us is for us." He is the Christ of the open heart.

Christ Settles Us "at Home"

Second. An open heart produces an open mind. In worship we regularly rehearse what we have heard before. Creed, hymn, text, prayer. In this practice, Christ settles us again so that we have that "at home" feeling about life.

Of all the losses in our time, it is this loss of feeling at home in life that is most crippling. Before 9/11 we knew were east of Eden. Culturally now we are Far East of Eden. But Christ -those not against me are for me—settles us to the sense of being at home.

I know there is a hard side to feeling homesick. Yet Frederick Beuchner once used that sensibility as a description of faith. We long for home. When we settle in, when we feel a little confident, when we enter the presence of the Master, and sup at his table, then we can do all things through Him who welcomes us!

When we feel "at home", in Christ, then we gain the freedom of the open mind.

---

2. Matthew 12:30.

I love the story of Hiawatha. 500 years ago this Onondogan taught five warring tribes a lesson: "he who is not against us is for us." The Iroquois confederacy was born and lasted to the Revolution, along these same lakes. Longfellow had some of the history wrong, and his language is archaic, but even now you feel he had his pulse on the truth of Hiawatha's song:

> *By the shores of Gitchie Gumee*
> *By the shining Big Sea Water*
> *Stood the wigwam of Nokomis*
> *Daughter of the Moon, Nokomis*
>
> *All your strength is in your union*
> *All your danger is in discord*
> *Therefore be at peace henceforward*
> *And as brothers live together*
>
> *Sat the little Hiawatha;*
> *Heard the whispering of the pine-trees,*
> *Heard the lapping of the waters,*
> *Sounds of music, words of wonder;*
> *'Minne-wawa!" said the Pine-trees,*
> *Mudway-aushka!" said the water.*
>
> *Saw the fire-fly, Wah-wah-taysee,*
> *Flitting through the dusk of evening,*
> *With the twinkle of its candle*
> *Lighting up the brakes and bushes,*
> *And he sang the song of children,*
> *Sang the song Nokomis taught him:*
> *"Wah-wah-taysee, little fire-fly,*
> *Little, flitting, white-fire insect,*
> *Little, dancing, white-fire creature,*
> *Light me with your little candle,*
> *Ere upon my bed I lay me,*
> *Ere in sleep I close my eyelids!"*[3]

It takes a sense of confidence, of being at home, to think and live in a new way. Especially if that open mind leads to a serious change. I agree too with Peter Marshall that if you don't stand for something you will fall for anything. There is also a danger to breadth. Still, the burden of the Christian Gospel leans more against the danger of the narrow and

---

3. Henry Longfellow, *Song of Hiawatha*, Electronic Text Center, University of Virginia Library.

the divisive and the exclusive than against the danger of the open and the broad.

To change and grow we need the confidence of a stable home. Our Bishop told once of children liberated from the concentration camps who even when they fed could not sleep, fearing that tomorrow hunger would return. Some GI had the happy thought of putting a loaf of bread in every child's hands at nightfall. They slept. They slept holding tomorrow's bread today. That is being at home, holding tomorrow's bread today.

It is fascinating that the only mention of John in the Gospel of Mark is here. The Gospel named for John is the most open minded of the four. In the teeth of trouble, John upheld the open mind of Christ. John faced two problems. He faced the theological problem of the delay of the parousia (the brute fact that contrary to the teaching of Jesus and Paul the end of the world was not at hand). He faced the religious problem of the challenge of Gnosticism.

It is astoundingly encouraging to recall that in the terrific disappointment of the loss of eschatological urgency in the second century, John discovered the courage to keep an open mind, and so he found the inspiration to celebrate not Apocalypse but Spirit. No other New Testament voice found the courage to do so. Matthew and Luke hid the delay of the end behind the missionary triumph of the church. The Montanists and Docetists took extreme side doors out. 2 Peter, an early creative accountant, introduced a new eschatological math, "one day for the Lord is 1000 years."[4] But John kept an open mind. He let go of one of three of four most cherished teachings of his inheritance: the nearness of the end of time. Oh, he kept the form and words here and there. One day, one day. But he celebrated Spirit and gave Apocalypse benign neglect.

And he found a completely new expression, a new language, for the Gospel. In the beginning was the Word. Would today he have written, "In the beginning was the Web?"

In our day, we need to keep an open mind, too. Some forms of Christian faith are no longer fit for a global village, and a spiritual village green. A narrowly exclusive expression of Christ, a cherished teaching from our inheritance, we must let go. Our faith in Christ, who settles us into our home, may be particular without being exclusive. Again, for all of his unfair enslavement to the opposing cause, it is John who best

---

4. 2 Peter 3:8.

expresses Gospel breadth. Is it unfair to wonder whether some of that breadth goes back in Johannine memory to this moment along the lake: "who is not against us is for us?" We need to hear the real John of the open mind: "The true light that enlightens everyone, *everyone*, was coming into the world." But did John's Christ not say, "I am the way and the truth and the life?"[5] Yes and by it he meant: wherever there is a way, there is Christ. Wherever you find truth, there is Christ. Wherever there is breath of healthy life, there is Christ. All who come home do so with these.

Christ Is Our Home

Third. The very Christ who brings us home and settles us at home is lastingly, finally our home. Our passage ends with a staggeringly universalistic promise of reward for any and all who have even slightly, even to the measure of a cup of water given, come alongside the mission of Christ. "They will not lose the reward." This is a reference to heaven. He is the door to heaven. He is the Christ of the Open Heart, the Open Mind and the Open Door. "I am the door. If anyone enters by me, he will come in and go out and find pasture."

In baptism we put on Christ. Already, by promise, water and spirit, we are home, beginning at baptism. Already, at baptism, we have drowned the Old Adam. Already, at baptism, we have faced our mortality and our selfishness. Already, at baptism, we have begun to reside in a house not made with hands, one in which there are many rooms. Lord, we may tarry here awhile, but we are going home.

Home.

One Monday, entering ministry, I remember a trusted mentor saying he had never in the ministry of faith ever seen anyone fear death. That gave me hope.

A Tuesday, years later, he said he did not fear death himself. He had some worry about getting there, but not the river itself. That gave me hope.

Then on a Wednesday, Henri Nouwen, now across the river, said he dreamed that at heaven he was greeted with an embrace, a question about his travels, and the phrase, "let's see your slides." That gave me hope.

---

5. John 14:6.

Thursday a phrase caught up to me, "I shall dwell in the house of the Lord forever." And S Jackson: "Let us cross over the river and rest in the shade of the trees." That gave me hope.

Friday morning, one birthday, I learned a man of my own age had died the night before. I thought how impossible it is for us to imagine the world without us, or to imagine ourselves apart from our world. We live, daily, in an imaginative bubble of temporary immortality. But I also remembered the phrase, "love is stronger than death." That gave me hope.

Saturday there was the memory of two boys playing trumpets, at evening, across the southern end of a Finger Lake. Call and response, Day is dying in the west . . . That gave me hope.

Come Sunday, that's the day. Now to stand under the gaze of another One, who brings home, who settles us at home, who is our lasting home, the Christ of the open heart, the open mind, the open door. Today in his presence—Christ is with us, lift up your hearts—He gives me hope.

HEADING HOME . . .

It was an early feminist theologian, Dorothy Gale, another Kansan, who rightly said, "There's no place like home." So true. He is our home. Are you heading home? Jesus said, "Who is not against me is for me." Are you against him? To announce a Gospel of freedom and grace we need preachers and laity who embody an existential capacity for grace and freedom. Who is not against me is for me. Are you for him? Faith is an act of personal commitment to an unverifiable truth. Will you live on his behalf? Will you live with an open heart and mind and door?

11

Hope

Mark 10:17-31

TO THE LAKE

JESUS MEETS US TODAY on the shoreline of real hope. At the edge of the water of life he invites us to wade out from the dry land of having and into the living water of giving. He is calling you from having to giving. He is inviting me to be a trustee of the future as well as the past. He is offering us a chance, a chance, a daily chance not only to conserve and protect but also to develop and enhance. Up here along the lakes.

The bright lights of a big city, Jerusalem or New York, may distract our attention from the 50% of Christ revealed along the lakeshore. Down south to Jerusalem the Jews went, including we may suppose those like Jesus and Mary and Joseph who lived 'upstate,' for great autumn and winter and spring festivals (Sukkoth, Hanukah, Passover), as we go south to the Big Apple for the great autumn and winter and spring festivals (Thanksgiving, New Years, Easter). Mark remembers Jesus teaching, though, along the lake of Genessaret. Lessons for living along the lakeshore: once more to the lake! The Gospel in a word today is hope, past and present and future. We have a heritage of hope. Jesus Christ, today's real presence, inspires hope. The future holds for us a collective hope.

We Have Heritage of Hope

In the first place, you are descendants of hopeful people.

Just to the north of Owasco Lake, in the historic section of Auburn, you may find time to visit the home of William Seward. Seward lived and practiced law along the northern shore of the lake. Unlike his Moravia neighbor, Millard Fillmore, he never became President, although he was the leader of the nascent Republican Party. He served as Secretary of State from 1861 to 1869, was nearly killed on the same day and by the same plan that took Lincoln, became a highly skilled international diplomat (how we could use his spirit today!), and was vilified in his own lifetime for an act of hope of uncommon proportion. William Seward, of the Finger Lakes, knew that hope is in the living water of giving not on the dry land of having, in the water of development not on the rocky shore of protection. He came from an upstate farm family, but he had the courage and genius to give, to generously invest in an unknown and unforeseeable future. More urbane leaders were more tepid. Not Seward. Like a poor woman with only a farthing to spend, he did spend; he did give, and did so with hope and grace. In a time of calamitous confusion—1867!—Seward bought Alaska for $7.2M, $2 an acre. For such courage he was persecuted and vilified. "Seward's icebox," the downstate press chortled. But his visionary generosity to the future, like that which built Asbury First, and that which will build our future, are gifts to an unknown future, and an unborn generation. Hope meets us at the shoreline of having and giving, at the point we wade out from conservation and protection into development and enhancement. Which brings us suddenly to Mark 10.

Jesus Inspires Hope

In the second place: Jesus the Faithful Presence inspires hope! In the city of Rome, under the thumb of Caesar, Mark in 70ad rehearses Jesus' lakeside lessons. Gathered in secrecy, hearing news of a Jerusalem temple in flames, rightly fearing impending persecutions, Mark's Roman Christians heard hope in these teachings, so frequently as today related to wealth. If you notice only one word in this passage, mark Mark's inclusion of "persecutions" (vs. 30).

For there is an urgency to Mark's passage that Matthew and Luke have left behind. Mark exudes raw energy under the pressure of apocalyptic expectation. Sell and give! Some will not taste death until they see the Son of Man. Notice the telltale apocalyptic marks: eternal life (the coming resurrection of the dead); this age and the age to come (the heart of Jewish longing); camel and needle (end of an age hyperbole); none is good but God (the apocalyptic distance of heaven from earth); the reign of God (the essential apocalyptic hope); persecutions (harbinger of the end); last become first (apocalyptic justice). But there is no mistaking the primary announcement: life is found in the lake of giving not on the shore of having. Yes, you must honor the past, including the commandments (though Mark's Jesus lists only the second 5). Yes, we must conserve and protect. But as LT Johnson told us this week: "the tradition of the church is meant to open the future!"[1] Conserve what you can and protect what you must, then give—develop, give—enhance, give—and open the reign of God! This is what life is all about.

At the end of this month's remarkable election in California, a Mexican American Democratic leader in L. A. memorably implored his people to look to the future: "Think of your future. Look to the next generation. See what is out ahead. Why if you vote for (candidate x) it would be like a chicken voting for Colonel Sanders!" He could speak apocalyptic.

Speaking of apocalypse and chickens, it is like the old story of the Methodist Ham and Egg dinner. A hen and a pig stopped in to the church and were so impressed by their welcome and welcoming space that they offered to help. The pastor saw the hen and pictured eggs. She saw the pig and pictured ham. "Well, we could use you both, but for one of you this would be a significant contribution and for another it would mean real sacrifice!" She could sing apocalyptic.

Jesus spoke more about money than about almost anything else. Here as elsewhere he offers a word of hope. Giving does most for the giver. Over a lifetime you will be happiest about what you give. You only possess what you can personally give away. What possesses you, and the rich young ruler, you do not want. You want freedom, the freedom to give.

It is hard not to be had by what you have. So the good news counsels, "Store ye not up treasure on earth . . ."[2] At a meeting Tuesday Tom Fassett quoted Wordsworth: "The world is too much with us, late and soon.

---

1. Luke Timothy Johnson, lecture notes.
2. Matthew 6:19.

Getting and spending we lay waste our powers. Little we see in nature that is ours. We have given our hearts away, a sordid boon."

Peter, the disciple whom Mark loved, provides the counter example to the possessed man. He has left everything and received everything. He has been inspired in Jesus the Christ to live in hope. Peter has found the hope to risk building a kingdom that does not yet exist. He is learning to swim on the lake of giving after standing for so long on the shore of having.

To learn to swim you have to trust that the water will hold you up. It will. We have a role as trustees of our church. All of us are trusted in our time with a future time. What becomes of this congregation in 2020 is being determined right now. As trustees we bear responsibility not only to conserve and protect the past but also and more so to develop and enhance the future. There is an irony here, too. The only way you can really conserve and protect the past is to develop and enhance the future. Like Jeremiah buying land as the city burned, Peter invested in faith as calamity overtook him. We can too. Let's. Jesus inspired hope in Peter and he can do so in us today. Which brings us upstate in 2003.

Ours Is a Collective Hope

In the third place, the good news gives birth, the Christian gospel gives birth, to the blood spattered, umbilically tethered, tiny cherub of hope, weekly, in its reading and hearing and interpretation. Over against our upstate economic malaise, we are forced by today's reading to consider the horizon of hope for our region. This passage lays hold not of what is wrong but of what is right!

Hope is not optimism. Hope is realism with ears and eyes. Finger Lakes New York is becoming poorer by the minute. I have clippings from this calendar year of manufacturing demise in Corning, Binghamton, Oneida, Syracuse, and Rochester. Glass, computers, silver, air conditioning, caskets, film—let us conserve and protect as much as we can. Hope, though, has ears for what the future is saying too. Not only to conserve and protect, but also to develop and enhance.

Hope is realism with ears. Hope hears the analysis and knows its partial truth: our infrastructure is too old; our schools are too rowdy; our elderly are too expensive; our taxes too high; our manufacturers do not speak Chinese (literally, figuratively, or monetarily); our cities are too rusty; our farms are too rocky. We would be better off downstate, in Jerusalem, or in Diaspora, in Texas.

Hope is realism with eyes, too. Eyes that see a new future being born. It is a good lakeside future! With God all things are possible. Be grateful for what you have been given and so give to the future in hope! Here are five fingers of hope, like the slim fingers of the lakes themselves that beckon us in hope.

You have an exquisite, glacially sculpted lakeside geography like no other. Flaunt it!

You have a tough, varied, post-modern meteorology, including snow and ice, like no other. Market it!

You have a progressive, human friendly, Rockefeller republican culture like no other. Cherish it!

You have a proven, compassionate, historically liberal political heritage. Support it!

You have a flourishing, ecumenical, broad spirituality more vibrant than nearly any world wide. Invest in it!

Geography, meteorology, community, history, spirituality. Not wealth, perhaps, but just maybe treasures akin to those of heaven. Enjoy, savor, and appreciate, live!

Have dinner at the Aurora Inn. Buy some skates. Or skis. Read Reynolds Price along a quiet lake. Look up Vaclav Havel in a local library. Make a reservation at one of the following: Chautauqua, St Bonaventure, the Abbey of the Genesee, Colgate Chapel House, Jordanville Russian Orthodox Monastery, New Skeete Priory, Stella Maris, Casowasco, Willard Chapel in Auburn. New York State is Spiritual Smorgasbord and some people are going hungry! Here is another: Join Asbury First. And tithe!

I want to conserve and protect all manner of our manufacturing past as much or more than any other. In Webster, the next word below manufacture is manumission. Our future in Upstate New York is spiritual, though. Not only manufacture but also manumission. Manumission: freedom, liberation, emancipation, the reign of God. It would not surprise Hiawatha, or John Dempster, or Frederick Douglass or Harriett Tubman or Franklin Roosevelt.

God has a different, more modest, yet truly wonderful purpose for upstate. We are maturing. We can move from achievement to enjoyment, from manufacture to manumission, from materiality to spirituality. In our lifetime. We will earn less. We will have more jobs per home. One said: "I know the economy is getting better and there are more jobs because I have three of them now, not just one." Well. The future will be different, but it will be good. This is the meaning in part of Mark 10: there is hope for our region.

CALL TO FAITH

We may be less comfortable with real hope than we are with real despair. Things are much easier, in one sense, if there is no hope or future. We have no responsibility, then. If our regional future, or even part of our future, lies in spirituality, religion, faith, manumission, then this church is center stage, across the Finger Lakes, for century 21. Then we have a leadership role to play. Then we really do need to invest in the future. Then hope will involve not only conservation and protection but also development and enhancement. No, the canal is not coming through, nor the railroad, nor the highway. That is the past. But a canal culture of natural grace? A railroad of personal freedom? A highway of spiritual emancipation? Everything north of Yonkers is one gracious beautiful garden. You have the good news to share that will help a future generation to get off the highway of having and get into the garden of giving.

I have a hope that you will hope too. It is the hope that the spiritual, Christian love I have known at Asbury First, in all its liturgical, didactic, and missionary excellence, will be available for my grand children. Growth always requires the risk of change. And not small change, either.

50 years ago this month ground was broken for our sanctuary. Your pastoral team and households are making a challenge commitment to build our future calculated to remember these 50 years. It is our hope that with Peter of old we together can step out from the dry land of having and wade in the water of giving.

I affirm the Finger Lakes and the Gospel of Christ has what it takes to open a future across upstate and a living faith on this very date.

12

Heart

Mark 10:35–45

WHO?

WHO TAUGHT YOU ABOUT power?

Who taught you by precept or example about the use of authority? Think for a minute, or for a good stretch of a lifetime, about those who modeled for you the spiritual dimensions of leadership. Unreflectively we follow their lead if reflectively we do not assess their example. And every one of us has power, exercises some authority, and leads, especially in our example.

Carlyle Marney used to ask us: "Friend, who told you who you are?"

The Gospel today asks of us a narrower question: who taught you about power? The Gospel today tells us that authentic authority, real responsibility are a matter of the heart. What are your models of power?

SHAKER SIMPLICITY?

Is one the heartfelt happiness of simplicity? Heartfelt leadership is ultimately very simple.

Said John Wesley, repeatedly, "if thine heart be as mine, give me thine hand."

And Calvin: What is chief purpose of human life? To glorify God and enjoy God forever.

There will come a day when you wake up to the purity of the heart that, as Kierkegaard said, is to "will one thing." That is conversion, often wrought in power struggle.

You may come to a morning hour, even this one, in which you sense a new opening, a desire to live a life that makes God smile. You will become kinder, happier, more generous, more forgiving. This is the purpose of being alive, to speak and act and be in a way that brings a smile to the divine countenance.

It is intriguing that the Gospel lessons about living, in Mark, are set in the humble reaches of the lake country. Writing in Rome in trouble in 70 CE, there must have some comfort, some folkloric encouragement for the persecuted urban Christians in these polished memories of Jesus teaching along the shores of Galilee. There is beauty along the lake. There is calm along the lake. There is peace along the lake. There is serenity along the lake. Along the lake there is space and time to sift, reminisce, remember, sort.

Who taught you what you know about power?

Along our lakes and rivers in this lovely region there arose a utopian sect, first in Albany and then in Cleveland, who embodied the simple life. In their work, their dress, their furniture, their devotion, their relations, the Shakers lived simply. The heart of their simplicity, and ours at our best, is the desire to "live a life worthy of the calling to which we have been called." Every renewal in Christian history has had this feature: Paul mending tents, Augustine chaste again, Luther and Erasmus cleansing Rome, Wesley and his coal miners, Latin American base communities, and every spiritual nudging in our own very human church.

Who are you trying to please? And how? And why?

Think of someone you have known who lived with a heartfelt, powerful simplicity.

Who taught you about authority?

AMBROSIAN AUTHORITY?

Is another model the heartfelt affirmation of the common good?

Mark 10:35 is one of the few spots in the earliest gospel at which the emerging institutional needs of the church are visible. Christianity wrestled with formational questions in the first century: For whom is the gospel? What are the definitive texts? And especially, who shall hold authority. What, How, Where. And Who.

As this passage shows, from the outset it has been terribly difficult for the Christian church to maintain its own authentic form of authority, over against the lesser models abroad in every age. I emphasize the little phrase, slave of all, or servant of the whole. "Knowledge puffs up, but love builds up," said Paul.[1]

We saw the film "Under the Tuscan Sun" last week. It was beautiful. Aristotle taught us to attend to the true, the good, the beautiful. In the late fourth century there emerged a good, great leader of the church, Ambrose of Milan. In just eight days he went from unbaptized layman to Bishop. His rhetorical skill, musicianship, diplomatic agility and attention to the preparations for Baptism provided the power behind his lasting influence in Northern Italy. Above all, Ambrose used his authority for the common good. Notice in the Scripture there is no avoidance of the need for leadership. Authority may be shared but responsibility is not to be shirked. What lasts, what counts, what is true and good and beautiful, finally, is what "builds up."

The greatest teacher of the earlier church, Augustine of Hippo, came to Milan a non-Christian. From the influence of Ambrose he left baptized and believing and worked a generation to set the foundations for the church over a thousand years to come.

I find some striking parallels to the story of Ambrose in a now popular book by Jim Collins, *Good to Great.* Here are the qualities of those in authority in companies that became great when they had before been good: quiet, humble, modest, reserved, shy, gracious, mild-mannered, self-effacing, understated, did not believe his own clippings—a plow horse not a show horse. A lot of progress can be made when we do not linger to long over who gets the credit.

Some years ago I went to a church meeting near Potsdam on a very cold night. It was led by our Bishop. For some reason I was not in a very happy mood, nor was I very charitable in my internal review of his remarks that evening. I do not recall his topic or theme. I remember clearly seeing him help to move hymnals, borrowed from other churches for the

---

1. 1 Corinthians 8:1.

large crowd, so they could be returned. Snow, dark, long arms carrying a dozen hymnals into the tundra.

Who taught you about power?

Think of someone you have known who lived with heartfelt passion for the common good.

Who taught you about leadership?

SERVANT OF SERVANTS?

Is another the example of deliberate and deliberative service?

Clint and I drove down through Ithaca in July. It was wonderful. Our two older kids were born there but I really have not been back in over twenty years. I believe there is a physical dimension to mind, to memory and maybe even to hope. It is important to be in certain places in order to receive certain insights, past and maybe even future. That is why reunions can be so powerful. Forgotten familiar spaces can evoke long buried memories. (It happens that just as this sermon was finished yesterday, a group of Doublers came to visit their former classroom next door to my office.) I remembered powerfully the experience of discovering, in a simple pamphlet in the Ithaca library, the graduate program that would form 10 years of our lives in Montreal. It was one of those uncanny moments when you feel that something beyond you is taking you by the hand and putting you somewhere.

Going north meant that I would not learn from Charles Rice at Drew. But I followed him through the years. A few years ago he spoke about the servant of the servants of God. He told about an Easter when he was in Greece. He sat in the Orthodox Church and watched the faithful in devotions. There was a great glassed icon of Christ, to which, following prayers, women and men would move, then kneel, then as they rose they kissed the glassed icon. Every so often a woman dressed in black would emerge from the shadows with some cleanser, or windex, and a cloth and –psh, psh—would clean the image, making it clear again. And he had a revelation about service and power and authority and leadership. And through him I did too. Maybe it will work for you. As he watched the woman in black cleaning the icon, he realized that this was what his ministry was meant to be. A daily washing away from the face of Christ all that obscured, all that distorted, all that blocked others from seeing his truth, goodness and beauty. Including a lot of piety. Service that lasts is deliberate and also deliberative, it is body and mind.

My friend Henry told me a while ago that when his new leader came he helped the man put on an old frayed black robe. But by the time he retired, the man was wearing a white, purple, ostentatious gown. Henry felt like something had been lost.

This last week I attended an annual meeting through which I saw again the freshened image of Christ in the person of our host. For a year he sent, monthly, carefully crafted letters about various aspects of our gathering, both to novices and "grizzled veterans" as he said. These epistles were beautiful overtures to the event to come. A month before the meeting he directed his staff to telephone those who had not fully finalized their plans. That would include delinquent me. He prepared lodging and meals, program and transportation. Every day those in attendance received a bag of information, treats and jokes. On the first day he spoke, at our beginning, with brevity and power about the need for attention to detail in our work. He spoke personally about his own father and some of the issues of authority and power there, and also of his own son who had died of suicide at age thirty. He did not shirk responsibility and yet he did not horde authority. He set the beat and guided the conversation, no mean feat with thirty preachers and no agenda. He was up early with the details of hosting and stayed late for those last minute conversations. Every so often he inserted a brief, but telling comment to highlight or shade another's thought. On the last day, he again spoke, before the Holy Communion, again with brevity and power, about Real Presence. He offered a prayer of consecration, broke the loaf and raised the chalice and placed them on the table, then stood back inside the circle saying, "no one need hold this." We came one by one to bread and cup, prepared by a servant of the servants of God.

Think of someone you have known who provided heartfelt service to the servants of God.

Who taught you about power?

CODA

Every one of us has some power. If you have a pen, a telephone, a computer, email, a tongue, a household, a family, a job, a community, a church—then you have some authority.

Who taught you, by precept and example, how to use it? How much of what you picked up needs keeping and how much needs to be put out on the curb?

A simple passion for the common good of the servants of God is at the heart of leadership.

For the Son of Man came not to be served, but to serve, and to give His life as a ransom for many.

13

Habit

Mark 12:28–34

LOVE IS . . .

Skaneateles Lake runs south ten miles past Mandana and New Hope and Scriba, to rest in embrace of the Allegheny plateau. Down there some years ago a man told how he came to faith:

It was in those years of too few dollars and days, and too many deliveries and diapers. We seemed to be always at odds, kids crying, not a dollar or an hour to spare. I had signed up for a morning prayer group in our church, every Wednesday. It got that I dreaded going. I was tired; the meeting was chaotic, attendance spotty. I like things done right. One morning I didn't go. The next Wednesday my wife kneed me out of bed. Our deal was to pray and then to take a card from a pack the pastor had of service needs. So I took mine: "Boy needs ride to Sayre Hospital tomorrow." That was the straw, or almost the straw: "this is a whole day, not an hour—I didn't sign up for this!" I huffed out. Sometimes though after I blow off some steam I think different. That little card rode around in my jacket during work. When I got home I made the mistake of telling my wife about it. She didn't say anything, but she had that look and that jaw set back and that, you know that attitude. About 11pm I called the home and said I'd take the boy.

Early Thursday I drove across town. He was already there on the curb, alone and with a little suitcase. I was still so frosted about the whole thing I just kept silent for a while. I watched him though from the corner of my eye. He took some cookies from the bag and offered me one. He watched the scenery. I saw him read a note that was wrapped around the cookies. He was about five. With our four girls I realized I didn't have much practice at talking to a boy. After a while he told me about his leg. It was something he was born with. The operation was going to help him walk right. They had to postpone it until his mother got work again. She had just gotten another job and was so grateful. Then he asked me the most surprising thing I have ever been asked: "Mister, are you God?" He asked so sincerely that I stifled my laughter and asked what he meant. He said:

"Last night after dinner I got ready for bed. My mom was really upset. She said she had to go to work today or we would lose our house, but that I had to get to the hospital or my leg would not ever be right. She came into my room and prayed, 'God please help us. God please take my boy to the hospital. God help us somehow for tomorrow.' When I got up this morning she told me God was helping us. So that is why I asked you: Are you God?"

You ask how I found my faith? I found my faith by practicing my faith.

Virtue is formed by habit. Faith is formed by practice. Habits form virtue. Practices form faith.

Said the tourist to the violinist, at 50th and 9th Ave, "How do I get to Carnegie Hall?" "Practice, practice, practice..."

You would like to have self-control? Practice restraint.

You would like to be gentle? Speak gently.

You would like the gift of faith? Act faithfully.

You would be good? Do good.

You want to become kind? Live kindly.

You desire patience? Practice the arts of prayer.

You hunger for peace? Live peaceably.

You hope for joy? Sing and practice singing.

And love? One who would know love must love others.

Here is what the Greek word *agape* means: self-giving. What becomes habitual with us becomes us. This ancient text asks us to compare our habits with love.

Dr. Lohmeyer long ago, rightly in my view, identified the original setting of this controversy story along the Sea of Galilee. Its positive depiction of the Pharisees, its rough directness in speech, its colloquial character, and its willingness to see Jesus receive the praise of his Jewish neighbors all argue so. The careful readers among us will note that Mark already has us in Jerusalem. Yet the original setting for this crucial teaching on love was, probably, the lakeshore. No surprise. Half the gospel happens upstate.

A powerful summary of the law is here rendered for the first time in history. How are we to live? By loving God and loving our neighbor. Who first connected Deuteronomy and Leviticus? Mark? The early church? Jesus? All we can say is that we have the teaching as our Word of God.

As Flip Wilson's Geraldine told her\his boyfriend Killer: "What you see is what you get." The gospel in a word is love. And what is love?

Commitment

First, love is commitment. If you thought you would escape this service without hearing the word 'commitment' you are about to be disappointed. For when the Bible speaks of love it really means to speak of commitment. Commitment implies staying power, the power to see things through, the lasting strength that carries you beyond a valley to the next hill, beyond sickness to future health, beyond poverty to future wealth. Commitment in youth. Commitment, if God so blesses you, for children. Commitment through middle-age. Commitment as you take your places as working, caring members of the community. Especially a commitment to grow old in community. Then as the gray hairs multiply you will begin to see what love can mean. For "in this is love, not that we loved God, but that God loved us." No mere infatuation this. For if God had been merely infatuated, how quickly he would have given up on us. Rather it is God's own commitment that directs and encourages us to mimic him.

It may seem odd to quote the newest Californian, by the way easily the finest governor that professional bodybuilding ever produced. But I will. Asked how he could possibly manage a job like the one he now has he said: "I think it is like body building. First comes the commitment."

Virtue is formed by habit, faith by practice.

We have sometimes worn better men's clothes to become better men.

A judge wears a robe not because he is less human than we but because, being equally human, he needs to pretend to a higher wisdom. Children dress up on Halloween not because they are less human than we, but because, being equally human, they need to pretend to a greater imagination. Clergy wear vestments not because they are less human than others but because of the opposite, being equally human we need to pretend to a fuller spirit. Brides and grooms wear tuxedos and gowns not because they are already mature but, to the contrary, because they know their human limitation on the one hand and the mountainous nature of the commitment they are making on the other. So they dress up. So at least they can look the part. So they can pretend and—here is the point—by pretending, prepare, and by preparing, become . . . faithful.

Do all the good you can . . . And over time you just might become—good. In our church it is time to hear the wedding bells for the Bride of Christ. In this congregation we have plenty of courtship, some serious dating, even some engagements in faith. But there are some cold feet out here this morning. Now it's time to come to the altar and tie the knot and make some commitments. I tell you, they will be the making of you. Faith is formed in the practice of faith.

I am told of a man stranded for a decade on a desert island. At last a ship came by and rescued him. The ship captain saw three buildings carefully made and asked about them. "The first is the house I live in." And the second. "The second is the church I attend." And the third. "The third is the church I used to attend." Isn't it time we settled in and made this our real home? To do that takes commitment.

Delight

Second, love also means delight. Times of sheer delight will come upon you when you least expect them. Take the time to savor them! They are meant to give you strength. Yes, the groom's delight as he sees for the first time his bride's beauty as she appears before him in the wedding gown. After some time together, the delight of a shared glance across a crowded room—perhaps a reception or party—as friends and partners in an instant know without speaking what is in each other's minds. Let us warn you that life is not chock full of delight. For some the moments of delight are few and far between. But they come to us all. When they come, take the time to savor them. And hope that God on occasion even delights in us, his creatures. "For God so delighted in us that he sent his Son, that whoever believes in him might not perish, but have eternal life."

What clouds our native delight is the accretion of what the Scripture calls sin. Sin has many forms, but all of them mar the delight of the day.

Our besetting adversary in Rochester, NY in 2003 is a pervasive spirit of entitlement. I breathe therefore I am. I exist and so I deserve. I live and so I expect. Our sin is a sense that life owes us. Something.

The economic sword of Damocles now hovering over us will cleave neatly, like Hitler through the Sudetenland, through generations of sloth and will burn out, like wildfire in San Diego, our besetting sense of entitlement. We will go backward in time. We will have to move 100 years into the past and 100 miles out into the lake country to recall the innovation, the risk, the frugality, the industry, the generosity, the commitment that built our home here. We will return to a time of hard work, modest income, limited budgets, requisite sobriety, daily gratitude, community spirit and the delight that comes daily with love. No, I do not relish the prospect. Its individual hurts, present in some measure this morning, I mourn and abhor. But there is one communal development that comes, if we will work with it together, from recession and trouble: a gradual spiritual movement from entitlement to gratitude.

Love has a way of delighting us. Remember Paul at his best?
Let love be . . . genuine!
Hate what is . . . evil!
Hold fast what is . . . good!
Love one another with . . . mutual affection!
Outdo one another in . . . showing honor!
Never lag in . . . zeal!
Be ardent in . . . spirit!
Be patient in . . . tribulation!
Be constant in . . . prayer!
Contribute to the needs of the . . . saints!
Practice . . . hospitality!

Wonder

Third, love is wonder. God so wondered at the world's possibilities that he gave his only Son, that whoever believes in him might not perish, but have eternal life.

"The world does not lack for wonders, but only for a sense of wonder." G K Chesterton, poet, playwright and Englishman, had it right, as he usually did: we long for a rekindled sense of wonder. From Shakespeare to Tennessee Williams to right now: what this world needs is a sense of wonder!

And for this rebirth of wonder, this new rebirth of wonder, we come to worship

This gracious and lovely space itself inspires wonder.

The music, choral and organ and solo and congregational does too.

So do the sturdy lines of venerable liturgy, hundreds of years in use, by kings and commoners alike, all who knew, as John Wesley said of himself, "how to prize the liberty of an Englishman."

We are certainly heartened by such a gathering, too.

Sometimes I scratch my head and wonder, in a more reflective way, about what is becoming of life. I see women and men plunging headlong into existence, and laboring under heavy yokes. I work therefore I am. I earn therefore I am. I earn therefore I am. I have therefore I am. I control therefore I am. I think therefore I am. But the great Apostle to the Gentiles warns us about all these and more. They will cease. When we finally hear that, we pause, as we do right now. And when we do, we are truly thankful for those who keep hope alive, those who keep drama alive, those who keep dreams alive, those with a sense of wonder.

For much of life we end up seeing what we expect to see. I do so every day. I need the reminders that come and the blinders that go with wonder.

"You see things as they are and ask 'Why.' We dream of things that never were and ask, 'Why not?' My generation thought Bobby Kennedy had written the line, but he did not. Actually, he did something better, he lived it. Actually, he did something even better still; he gave the last full measure of devotion to it. What was that about love being giving not taking, giving not using? You truly have only what you fully can give away. No, the line comes from the hand of a great Irish playwright, GB Shaw: "you see things as they are and ask, 'why?' I dream of things that never were, and I ask, 'why not'? (repeat).

Sometimes I find myself leafing through the imaginary photo album of doubt, leaves, you could say, from the photo notebook of an untamed pastoral cynic. I wonder: just how much has the human race learned in one generation? I lament: Are we dreamers anymore? And then I come to church. And I feel a rebirth of wonder. You take the world and make it young again! I remember David Mamet's admonition: "Train yourself for a profession that does not yet exist. That is the mark of an artist—to create something that formerly only existed in his or her heart."[1]

Remember Robert Frost: "Yield who will to their separation, my object in living is to unite my vocation with my avocation as my two eyes make one in sight. Only where love and need are one, and the work is play for mortal stakes, is the deed ever really done, for heaven and the future's sakes."[2]

You see. The world does not lack for wonders. Love is wonder. Love is commitment and delight. And love is wonder. Wondrous Love! "It is the God who said, 'Let light shine out of darkness' who has shown in our hearts to give the light of the knowledge of the glory of God in the face of Jesus Christ.

GO AND LIVE

Yes, there is a sense in which every Sunday is a return to the altar where vows are taken and then lived.

I encourage you to tithe primarily because of what it will do for your character, your temperament, your personality, your spirit, your soul. And you can start today. Maybe you already made out your pledge card. But you can take another and add a zero. We will know which one to count.

Our habits form whatever virtues we have. Our practices form our faith. Do good until you become good. Preach faith until you have faith. This is what John Wesley, of all the Christian tradition, best taught.

At one of our seminaries their lived a professor and his wife who for many years, every Sunday evening, gathered a group of young clergy for dinner. The dinner began at 5pm and their table was always full. After retirement his mind left him, and she lived the 36hr a day illness, which some in this room know far better than I. As he weakened his students would come to visit. He muttered unintelligibly, listening hardly at all. His wife explained, offered tea, and graciously received the prayers of her visitors. Through such an hour the professor made no sensible statement, a stunning reversal for such a brilliant teacher. His mind was gone. But not his heart and not his faith, formed in years of practice. As the visitor was about to leave he would stiffen, sit formally forward, his eyes would brighten, and his own voice would return, as with earnest deliberation he

---

1. David Mamet, *Writing in Restaurants* (New York: Random House, 2003), 181.
2. Robert Frost, *The Poetry of Robert Frost* (New York: Holt, 1974), 419.

would say, as he had for fifty years prior, "My wife and I are glad to have met you. We would be ever so pleased if you would be our guests this Sunday, for dinner. Come to our home at 5pm. You will honor us with your presence."

Virtue is formed by habit, and faith by practice.

14

Hand

Mark 12:38–44

HANDS FREE

On August 28th I left my car for servicing outside Hamilton, and took a long morning jog through the little lands of my hometown.

Lights were on already at the newspaper office, the Mid-York weekly, a dubious publication, begun in 1828. Four men were drinking coffee at McDonald's. I saw a dad walking hand in hand with a four year old daughter, who had in her hand a teddy bear.

This matter of hands deserves some thought. Hands once held now let go. Handlebars once gripped now are balanced by knees. Handshakes and handclasps replace the teddy bear of childhood. Is God's hand upon us? Are we in God's hand? If Jesus, "by the finger of God" does mighty works, are we ready again to be his hands?

THE HAND OF GOD

A friend flew me across our region some years ago. We took off from Rochester. We followed the Genesee. We flew east and then north. They do look like fingers, Canandaigua and Keuka and Seneca and Cayuga and Owasco and Skaneateles and all. They do. But fingers imply a Hand! And here in hand is today's gospel: in Christ we are in God's hand, Christ is

God's hand and those opening their hands in Him (like the poor widow) are also God's hand. This is the word in a word today: Hand.

Drive, fly, across our region. The hand of God is upon us, blessing us, opening out a future for us, loving us, touching us, helping us! The hand of God is upon us in slim fingers that beckon us into God's future.

At the south end of Cayuga Lake there is a college. I forget the name just now. You know that one famous alumnus is EB White, the writer. Like Mark composing the words of Jesus a generation later, White went back to his notes from English 101 and composed still the best book on writing in American English, *Elements of Style*, by transposing his teacher's lectures. Did William Strunk say "omit needless words" or was it White? Did Jesus say "she has given more than all the others" or was it Mark? Did William Strunk say "vigorous writing is concise?" or was it White? Did Jesus say, "she has given her very life" or was it Mark?

I honor White and the lakes and the hand of God upon us today and this fall. Read his story, about love and death and opening your hand to the future. It is called: "Once More to the Lake." It is about that moment when you realize that you do not have all day. I think the widow of Mark 12 so realized: That Rome was not built in a day, but it was built. That it is a great life but few of us get out alive. That there are things that need doing and saying. That our hands, too, are meant for freedom and grace and open life. I think his little story, "Once More to the Lake" is the finest I have ever read.

Look at this beautiful land we have been given. The Hand of God, from Canandaigua to Skaneateles, the Hand of God is upon us!

HAND TO HAND

Running again, I saw that someone had bought Hogg's house and needed a dumpster to clean out the attic. Seven Oaks was busy I could see at various points. The Robert Trent Jones course winds its hidden way around the back side of town and college. Of course I had to use the willow walk. And ascend library hill. And admire the quad. And notice that the artesian well is buried.

Coming down the hill I had a religious experience. This happens to me, running through town, and running through the stereoptic, bifocal experience of hurting jogger's knees in 2003 and bright happy memories of 1963 which, I must say, of the two, knees and memories, the memories were more *present*.

THE LAND OF THE OPEN HAND

And I was thinking of you and this fall. I had a desire to see the Gospel of Mark interpreted for our time and especially our setting, along the lakes of our region, so strikingly similar they are to the Sea of Galilee. More: I wanted to preach the full Christ of grace and freedom with you again. In love. Not some partial version from loony left or rowdy right, but the Name that is above every Name, Jesus Christ. The Christ of Gospel and Lake, of Heaven and Earth.

Christ is our Health: before this Healer your health matters! Christ is our Height: He asks of us a certain height so when at times the mob is swayed to carry praise or blame to far we may take Him as our star to stay our minds on and be staid! Christ is our Home: he makes open space, heart and mind and door for us and all by saying, "whoever is not against us is for us!" Christ is our Hope: he gives us realism with eyes and ears and inspiration to enter a new future in our region of glacial geography, exciting meteorology, progressive community, compassionate history, flourishing spirituality! *The Finger Lakes are the place to be, right in the Palm of God's Hand!* Christ is our Heart: whoever first taught you about power, Christ fixes power in the heart of those who with Him have a passion for the common good! Christ is our habit: virtue is formed by habit and faith by practice, practice, practice! Accept no thinner substitute! Accept the full Christ of health, height, home, hope, heart, habit, and, last, hand.

HAND OFF

Meanwhile, back on the jog . . .

It was a jolt to "wake up" running downhill from Colgate Chapel House and straight into the tidal arrival of the class of 2007. Tuesday, August 28th, 2003, 8:45am.

It was a majestic scene, worthy of Pickett's charge, VE day, Palm Sunday, Dunkirk, the Crusades, Wolfe at Quebec, Napoleon at Waterloo, or the night Bill finally leveled with Hillary. A collision.

Picture this. A parent and child carrying together a used TV and luggage. Twenty sophomores with light blue tee shirts reading, "Welcome frosh." A small jet flying into Hamilton International. One coed carried like a latter day Chinese princess on a rickshaw, in the backseat of an Oneida city cab. Fraternity boys running up the street with a makeshift "we love Colgate" banner. Sorority girls leading an Indian signal, the "Rebecca Chopp" (Chopp, A UM clergy, and St Paul School of Theology graduate, is President of Colgate). Two streets full of fine, fine automobiles. From the south, up from Binghamton on 12B, largely with New Jersey plates rolled Cadillacs, Beemers, Audi's Lincolns. From the north, down from Utica on 12B, largely with Connecticut plates rolled Porsches, SUVs, high end Buicks, MGs. For once there was a traffic jam in Hamilton.

Without exception, vehicle to vehicle, the future Red Raider was asleep in the back seat. Dad was looking at the side view mirror. Mom was weeping. I found myself weeping too. One had to in the sight of this apocalyptic liminality. One woman, dressed in black, and perched on the curb seat side of a black SUV, was weeping uncontrollably, like Rachel of old.

WIDOW'S HAND

Tears bring us together. Abraham Heschel: "Different are the languages of prayer, but the tears are the same." In Rome, under the thumb of Caesar, Mark has focused our attention on a poor widow's hand as it opens above an offering box. We, Church, Mark, Jesus, All have paused for this Gospel moment, to observe the opening of a withered hand. Gathered in secrecy, hearing news of the toppled Temple, fearing impending persecution, the Roman Christians saw again the hand of God reflected in the courageous open hand of a poor widow.

This is a stylized story, a cookbook catechesis. Mix in one part each: teaching setting, Jesus, criticism of the Scribes, reference to money, and a single earth shattering word. Stir. Serve hot on Sunday. This widow saw something and gave her guts to it, "her whole life."

I have a bone to pick with our NRSV at this point. The original does not say she put in her living or all she had to live on. No one can live on a farthing anyway. It says she put in her whole life. Βιος . . . βιος . . . βιος. Biology, Biosphere, Biodegradable . . . Life. She opened her hand and put her whole life on the nose of an invisible future. You have to have the gift of faith to open your hand to give and bless and let go.

God's hand in the Finger Lakes is not a fist, not a grip, not a clap, not a curse. God's hand is open. To give, to bless, to let go. That is the hand of love. That also is the hand of the poor widow. Like God, she has given everything, even her *whole life*.

We mishear the Scripture so often because we moralize when we should theologize.

It is only our patronizing attitude toward her—fed from the polluted springs of victimhood feminism and arrogant patriarchy both—that keeps us from the Gospel. In this story, the Widow is God!

Where did we ever get the idea that older women are powerless? Widows fed Paul. Widows funded Mark. Widows fomented three cataclysmic Christian progressive movements in the 19th century Finger Lakes. Widows fund the Women's Division of the UMC today. Widows, 'babushkas', kept the Russian Orthodox church open from Lenin to Gorbachev, from Proletariat to Perestroika. The story of the widow's hand is the story of God's hand, opening out in Christ to give, to bless, to let go.

Here is her hand, the divine hand in Jesus' teaching: letting go as one dining center guest did this week of money; letting go as she sometime did of spouse; letting go as she may have, in cruciform love, of her children. If you love somebody, you have to open your hand and let them go. This is the whole teaching of the Trinity: Father letting go Son, Son letting go Spirit, Spirit letting go church.

This widow has the courage and generosity to place her life on the nose of an invisible future. She has the courage to build something that does not yet exist. She has the guts to open the hand and execute. She hopes in the teeth of calamity. She gives to a temple that Mark knows is in flames. Is she related to Jeremiah?

HAND OF CHRIST

Meanwhile, back on the trail . . .

At the swan pond I stopped beside a similar woman and her ten year old son, who, with me, were watching the invasion. This is what I heard the poor woman and her impoverished son say. Or, this is what I think I heard. Or, what I imagine was said. Or, what could possibly have been said.

B: Mommy, what is all this?

M: Ah, it is *college* day son. The new ones are here.

B: Oh Mom look how sad it all is. College must be a terrible thing, like having your tonsils out. Everyone is crying.

M: Ach, faith and begorrah, son, you don't know a fiddler's finger about what you are saying. College is wonderful! You will go one day.

B: Ah, no Mam. I'm going to hold your hand. It looks terrible. Look at that woman there. She's older than you and not so pretty either. Her face is all red and fat with crying. See. College is awful. It must be or they wouldn't be crying so.

M: For the love of St Patrick, son, college is wonderful, it is a pot of gold at the rainbow. Listen. In college you will have your very own room.

B: Really. Mam, that sounds good.

M: And a TV all your own and you watch whenever you want.

B: You mean I don't have to do my homework after dinner like at home?

M: Well . . . You . . . No . . . You have to do your homework. But you can eat whenever you want and the food is so wonderful. Your Uncle Francis went to college at 100lbs and he weighed 280 at graduation.

B: You mean they have second helpings every night?

M: Every night son, every night. And you can eat whatever you want.

B: You mean not just macaroni and cheese and corned beef and cabbage?

M: Ach, son, this is what I tell you, you don't know what you're talkin' about. You can have meat and seconds and ice cream at every meal.

B: You mean hot dogs and hamburgers?

M: Yes. And *steak*.

B: What is steak?

M: Ah, steak is like hamburger dressed up for Easter Sunday, you'll love it. It tastes like sweet heaven and melts in your mouth.

B: But every one will want some—there won't be enough.

M: Son, you are getting on my nerves. You don't get it. In college it is like an Emerald heaven. There is always plenty. No macaroni. No lack of seconds. But . . . To go you have to get a *scholarship,* so you keep doing your homework.

B: What is a scholarship?

M: Don't they teach you anything at that Kendrick Ave School? A scholarship is like Christmas, like the angels touching earth, like the St Patrick's Day.

B: Look at these cars Mam, I don't recognize any of them. They're not like ours or the Risley's. They're big. And new. And the windows are all dark. There's no red rust on their doors. What is that?

M: You spell it C_A_D_I_L_L_A_C. It is the name of an Indian chief.

B: Do you think I could go to Colgate?

M: Ach, son, you will get a scholarship to the greatest Universities in the world. You will shake your feet from the dust of Colgate. You will go to Harvard or Oxford or Yale or Tubingen or Princeton or Salamanca or, if you are really lucky, Ohio Wesleyan.

B: Mam, what is that shirt like thing the big woman is wearing? It looks like clothes, but it doesn't cover her.

M: That is the devil's own work, avert your eyes. That is a *halter top*.

B: Ah, a halter top. That's what Father says he loves about summer, the halter top. He says he kissed the calendar on July 1, the birthday of St Halter.

M: That Father of yours should be horsewhipped for saying such things.

B: Mam, if college is so good, why are they weeping?

M: Well son, you know, to grow you have to leave and move and change and let go of your mother's hand. There is no growth without change and there is no change without leaving. And there is no leaving without letting go of the hand. It is the way of life. Things and people who don't change, who won't let go, they die.

B: Mam, school starts Tuesday. Coach Franklin says I need new sneakers. And Mam, Mam, Craig and Kris are going to play hockey this year. I am the second biggest boy in the class after Andy Migonis and they want me to play wing. But I need skates.

M: Ach, son, skates are expensive. We have you and your sisters and come October a little brother maybe and wouldn't you rather have a baby brother than skates?

B: If you say so Mam. I guess so. Maybe I can have skates next year. Maybe I can play hockey next year.

M: Maybe, son, maybe next year. But I am going to leave you now. St. Mary's and the Methodist church are having their sale. I know they have sneakers, and your size too.

B: High tops?

M: High tops, and some shirts, too, they had, and a new pair of pants and a good heavy coat and some golashes . . .

B: I don't like golashes.

M: . . . and a raincoat and if we're lucky Mrs. Howe will save us Byron's sport coat for church. And speaking of Mrs. Howe, I have a surprise. In their book bin I saw *Huckleberry Finn,* and I had her keep it out for you. If you finish your chores early, you can spend all the afternoon reading it and won't your sisters be jealous!

And she took his hand, and she let it go. And God takes our hand and God lets us go.

PART 3

Empire Spirit

15

New York

The View from Ellis Island

Exodus 14; Philippians 1

A DREAM OF DELIVERANCE

THE VIEW FROM ELLIS Island is your best perspective on 9/11. That is, the joyful memory of past deliverance gives the power to withstand current confinement. True for Moses, for Paul, for you, for all. It is the view from Ellis Island that saves after 9/11. About 15 years ago, when the Carousel Mall was still new, a religious temple built, and now being rebuilt, for the gods of getting and spending and laying waste of powers, 400 people gathered in the Mall's top floor room, to enjoy breakfast, the view, and the featured speaker, Mario Cuomo. He began with light banter, wondering how in the midst of state recession the local developers had found the capital to build, and teasing them about 'looking into it'. He told about meeting President Reagan for the first time. As he crossed the room to be introduced the jolly President said, 'You have no need to introduce this man. I would know him anywhere. A great American, leader, and Italian American. I am proud to greet Lee Iacocca at any time'. He spoke knowingly about the needs of central New York, but also had to spend time acknowledging the shortcomings that soon would bring his defeat.

He began at 8:20 and I did not look at my watch until 9:15. I believe it is the most powerful public oration I have personally heard, and it was delivered without a single note. As George Eliot might have said: "ingenious, pithy and delivered without book."

He concluded by talking, as he had in 1984, about Two Cities, one set on a hill, and one set far below. Two Countries, one rich and one poor. Two Nations, one for the many well to do, and one for all the others—the poor, the frail, the elderly, the disinherited, the minority. Two Realities, as different as night and day. After Katrina, his words sound very contemporary. You can hear his voice in the magic of the internet, twenty-one years later:

Ten days ago, President Reagan admitted that although some people in this country seemed to be doing well nowadays, others were unhappy, even worried, about themselves, their families, and their futures. The President said that he didn't understand that fear. He said, "Why, this country is a shining city on a hill." And the President is right. In many ways we are a shining city on a hill.

But the hard truth is that not everyone is sharing in this city's splendor and glory. A shining city is perhaps all the President sees from the portico of the White House and the veranda of his ranch, where everyone seems to be doing well But there's another city; there's another part to the shining city; the part where some people can't pay their mortgages, and most young people can't afford one; where students can't afford the education they need, and middle-class parents watch the dreams they hold for their children evaporate.

In this part of the city there are more poor than ever, more families in trouble, more and more people who need help but can't find it. Even worse: There are elderly people who tremble in the basements of the houses there. And there are people who sleep in the city streets, in the gutter, where the glitter doesn't show. There are ghettos where thousands of young people, without a job or an education, give their lives away to drug dealers every day. There is despair, Mr. President, in the faces that you don't see, in the places that you don't visit in your shining city.[1]

It was a striking kind of sermon to deliver, at the height of economic wellbeing in that part of the state, a sort of Robin Hood homily for the

---

1. Mario Cuomo, *Speech to the Democratic Convention*, 1984.

Sheriffs of Nottingham in the Carousel Mall. I only cried once, at the end, when he talked about his mother coming to this world across Ellis Island.

"The young Italian woman and her small child stepped on U. S. soil for the first time at Ellis Island in New York harbor. The immigration official got her vital statistics and then asked her, "How much money do you have? "None," she said, "Maybe a few dollars."

"How much education do you have?" "Not much," she answered.

"What skills do you have for employment?" "None," she replied.

"What does your husband do?" "He works in New Jersey in the trenches," she said. "You mean he is a ditch digger?" he clarified. "Yes," she replied.

The official asked, "You are telling me that you have come to America, with no money, no education, no marketable skills, with a small son and a husband who is a ditch digger?" "What were you thinking?"

"I was thinking that my son will grow up here and be the Governor of New York State," said Mario Cuomo's mother."

That is the dream of Ellis Island, the spirit that made this state and country so great. That is the remembrance of our common faith, our confidence in a future, still as open and as terrifying as it was for a poor Italian woman, looking out at Manhattan and the Statue of Liberty. That is also, and very much so, the heart of Exodus 14 and Philippians 1, the cry of the heart for deliverance from tyranny. The place from which to view 9/11 is Ellis Island. The way to think about the tragic horror of the Twin Towers and the other unspeakable hurts of that day is by the faith of Jesus Christ, the Son of the same God who fought for the slaves of Egypt, and prevailed, the Son of the same God who broke the spiritual shackles of Paul of Tarsus, and prevailed. This is your faith. For at our best, this country has been the last best hope, a city set on a hill, a place of liberty and justice, not only for some, nor even just for most. And those who know what they have received, by the power of God, and the expanding circle of freedom that is the meaning of Jesus Christ, can see things clearly-- from Ellis Island. That is the great insight of our best history, sung by Emma Lazarus—keep all the fine things and people, give us the poor, and little faith, and see what we can do!

It helps to have a reminder of our faith, from the life and voice of someone, like Cuomo, who has known height and depth, poverty and wealth, how to be abased and how to abound. The sociologists call such an one 'status inconsistent.' Many early Christians, the first readers and writers of our New Testament, were 'status inconsistent,' too.

That is, beloved, to get to the far side of terror, to get past 9/11, and all manner of similar tragedy, we truly will need, together, to rely on the faith of Christ, and to take the long view, and to take the view of deliverance, as did the slaves in Egypt, as did Paul in prison, and has have you, when the chips were down. The joyful memory of past deliverance is the key to withstanding current confinement.

A DAY OF DELIVERANCE

Our passage from Exodus is the most important one in the Old Testament. It is so significant that it gets quoted in Joshua, rehearsed in Isaiah, remembered in Jeremiah, explored in the Psalms, and recited every Passover in the Seder meal. It is the basic frame on which the wonders and words of Jesus were understood in early Christianity. It is bedrock, hallmark, heart, core. The main thing. The one thing.

So it is somewhat surprising that surveys show that many do not know much about Moses, or the story just read of Moses, great Moses, leading his slave sisters and brothers in a great fleeing from Pharaoh.

Moses, as the story goes, hidden in the bulrushes, to be spared persecution, and was found and raised by the daughter of the great Pharaoh. That is about as 'status inconsistent' as it gets: an Israelite slave given the palace for his home. As a young man, worked in Midian to shepherd for his father in law, killed an Egyptian who opposed him, and suffered mightily the shame and hurt of his people. Moses rose up as a liberating leader of his people, and eventually led them out of bondage.

Up to the Red Sea they came, and the waters parted for them, returning to clog the wheels of the chariots of Empire. A paradigmatic power, not a naturalistic one, says Brueggemann, and he is right enough. God is not a meteorological manager, but meets us as the power of freedom scraping its way home in life. The memory of the Red Sea, now largely conceded to lie beyond any historical tracing, is the paradigm of our faith. God brings good out of evil. God sends grace to overabound sin. God opts for the poor. God makes a way when all you see is a wall of water. Are we not in a week when we can hear that? God is at work in the world, powerfully, to make and keep human life human, and your hands are doing that work. Out went the Israelites to the wilderness of Sinai, and down came the water that clogged Pharaoh's chariot wheels.

The chariot wheels of Empire sometimes do get stuck the mud. The chariot wheels of order and rank sometimes do find themselves mucked up. The chariot wheels of great governments sometimes do find themselves halted and stymied. Then you need leaders who are not horsemen but chariot experts. And then Pharaoh and Empire are made to face what otherwise could stay in the shadows. That we forget the poor to our own damnation. By apocalypse, this past week, the central lesson of the Bible—real religion is never very far from justice—by apocalypse we have had to face this again. You do not break the commandments, especially 1, 3, 6, and 8 with impunity. You are broken by them. We thought somehow that our neglect of the lower 15% would go unnoticed in the universe.

Have you taught your children to remember the commandments? (Here, recited). Life, over time, will teach them, but experience is such a harsh teacher. There are so many things it is better not to have to learn from experience.

We may want simply to recall the basic contours of the Christian life: Praise God in private and public by daily prayer and weekly public worship; Be faithful in deed and speech to your partners and spouses; Give away a tenth of what you earn each year. Worship God, Keep Faith, Tithe. This is what it means, at a basic level, to begin the Christian life.

We have learned 9 to 11 religious lessons for and from 9/11:

- Religion matters
- Real religion is never very far from justice
- Religious perspective about heaven matters greatly
- We are woefully under prepared to think about world religions
- Religion involves hatreds as well as loves
- Religion, good religion, deserves our best dollars and hours
- Religion needs our best attention
- The great visions of religious perspectives, the utopian horizons, need to fuel our imaginations
- All of life is religious—even anti-religious postures and perspectives are fully, even sharply, religious
- We are not viewed with esteem from all the corners of the globe
- We face, across the globe, a violent, angry enemy, whose designs will not be resisted merely by the singing of hymns.

The children of Israel remembered, as they composed these verses during the later captivity in Babylon, that the joy memory of past deliverance brings power to resist present confinement.

A DECLARATION OF DELIVERANCE

Another status inconsistent soul greets us from behind bars, this morning. He too, in a time of terror, would have us meet the morning with joy. He is now somewhere near the end of his life. Thessalonians, Galatians, Corinthians, and Romans are in the rear view mirror. His imprisonment—could it have been something he said?—is for the sake of the good news, says he. Remember where he is . . .

The slammer, the joint, the tank, the hoosegow, the calaboose, prison, jail, the big house, up the river, in stir, doing time. There is a reason that Matthew 25 marks this condition alongside hunger, nakedness, loneliness, and sickness. The great prisoners, Socrates, Paul, King, Sadat, find a loosening of their mental shackles even in the grey bar hotel.

It is the imagination that most needs loosening, when one is caught in prison. And the imagination is everything for the future. After 9/11, we determined upon a military course, one part of which has our chariot wheels mired in Iraq. Our action was preemptive, unilateral, imperial, unforeseeable, and in those measures stood alone, across our long history, in overt contradiction of inherited just war theory. Now the question is whether, as a people, we can summon the imaginative power to free up a shackled situation. Can we not wonder together, and imagine together, a shared resolution?

One alternative would be to return to these same temporarily jettisoned principles, and find our way back home through them. To foreswear any future preemption: to say clearly and repeatedly that we are not in the business as a people of attacking others who have not attacked us or others. To actively engage a multiplicity of nations and organizations of nations: to recognize that for all the layers of inertia, the UN—which is both Kofi Annan and Dag Hammarskjold—or something very like it is a necessary tool. To forcefully eschew any advantage of natural resource, even in a time of shortage: our hands must be clean of oil. To set a clear time line: go in, finish, get out, soon. The just war arguments have proven, tragically, to be the stronger. Perhaps, together, across the older divisions of whether we should have or shouldn't have gone, we may find our way home by observance of these centuries old principles. I believe we can. But I also believe we have about a year left, at most, to do so.

The phrase translated so weakly here, 'your sharing in the gospel', is one of my favorites in all of scripture. The RSV had it somewhat better, "the partnership of the Gospel," but the original is best, the koinonia of the gospel—the mutuality, conviviality, priceless and freeing community of the Gospel! My brother minister, Ken McMillan, used the phrase to define his whole ministry—the partnership of the Gospel. Ken gave me the proverb, *Plan for the worst; hope for the best; then do your most; leave all the rest!* He gave the best succinct advice for happiness in ministry: *care for your family first; preach with all you have; spare nothing in visitation—hospital, officey, home.* He gave us a great family, from Los Angeles, Doug and Carol Major. But mostly he gave the light of this verse.

Paul sits in prison. His deliverance is another view from Ellis Island. He remembers the joy of past liberation, the freeing kindness of his Philippians, and he finds a way forward.

A DISCOVERY OF DELIVERANCE

Our forebears in faith donned their faith in struggle. We all have our 'status inconsistencies.' You have too. You may want, this special Sunday, when we remember a time of terror, to recall one of those points in life where faith did see you through. Not your own belief, but faith, the faithful love of Christ Jesus. Faith finally is personal. It is worked out, in blood, and in fear and trembling. To be yours it must be yours. That is why the document soon to appear which records the dozen lay witnesses from this summer is so central to our life together.

Our one city, New York, harbors crystal treasures, from the Cloisters, to Harlem and its new Dinosaur Barbeque, to Central Park—the mother of all village greens, to Little Italy and Wall Street and Battery Park. Your children need to see the inside of the United Nations. They should ride the elevator of the Empire State Building. They should walk Fifth Avenue, and eat a pretzel. In the writing of this sermon, there were barely reigns enough to keep the multiple horses of memory from stampeding all over the remains of the message. It is too much. We owe debts of spiritual gratitude to Reinhold Niebuhr for wrestling down Harry F. Ward, to Abraham Heschel for exalting Amos, to William Sloane Coffin for fighting off fundamentalism, to Paul Tillich for love of culture. New Yorkers all.

A humbler, darkened spot will forever, however, hold most power in our life. In our second year of marriage, the last year of seminary, and Jan was with child, we learned a little about deliverance. I was employed as a night watchman on 122 St, the requirements for the job, ideal for study, being height, weight and an unpleasant disposition. One late night Jan called in terrific pain. Something was wrong. We took a cab to St. Luke's on 112 and Amsterdam. The doctor said to me, memorably, "I do not know how bad this is, whether she will make it, and especially whether the child (then 18 weeks or so) will either. Call your family." That night my theological education began, in truth. The whole range of study and life took on a completely different hue. Alone, early in the morning, I found myself is a humble, dark, spot, a pew in the back of the Cathedral of St. John the Divine. I prayed, if you can call it that. My mother in law came and made residence for a week. My classmates appeared, to me, to be on a different planet, and so, as well, for my teachers, with one exception. Gradually the hours passed, and more gradually deliverance came. The cyst was removed. Mother and child survived. Mother in law and son in law survived each other. We lived to another day, a different day. A quick move to an open, small church in Ithaca. Departure from a great city, a plan of further study, a range of some freedoms. Suddenly, all of the waves of responsibility—spouse, parent, pastor, neighbor—splashed ashore. And we made it out alive. This, too, is the view from Ellis Island, the long look forward into freedom following deliverance. The far side of terror. The new creation. New York, city of freedom for those in need, means for me a wife and daughter, a wife saved and a daughter given.

And in that sliver, as your experience also teaches, we know Moses, we know Paul, and we know the freedom for which Christ has set us free. There is something else in the remembered dawn light streaming through the windows of St. John the Divine. A sense, a confidence, that however the medical situation had concluded, somehow, someway, God would see us through.

A DECLAMATION OF DELIVERANCE

The place from which to view 9/11 is Ellis Island. You, people of faith, take your stand on the shores of deliverance, on the coastline of liberty, along the moving tide of freedom, in the great surf of salvation. Emma Lazarus's poem, in full, is your song. Sing it.

Not like the brazen giant of Greek fame
With conquering limbs astride from land to land;
Here at our sea-washed, sunset gates shall stand
A mighty woman with a torch, whose flame
Is the imprisoned lightening, and her name
Mother of Exiles. From her beacon-hand
Glows world-wide welcome;
Her mild eyes command
The air-bridged harbor that twin cities frame,
"Keep ancient lands your storied pomp", cries she
With silent lips. "Give me your tired, your poor,
Your huddled masses yearning to breathe free,
The wretched refuse of your teeming shore,
Send these, the homeless, the tempest-tossed to me,
I lift my lamp beside the golden door.

16

Albany

Crossing the Hudson

Philippians 1; Exodus 16

OPENING

THERE IS A MAJESTIC bridge spanning the northern Hudson river as you drive west into Albany, a thin whisker of a bridge overcoming a great chasm—like the narrow gate, and the straight way that lead to life, and to the difference between the good and the great, and between the almost true and the truth. We call you today to cross over the river! Leave the east bank of the good for the capitol region of the great!

These rivers of freedom running across our state carry majestic chords of memory, as well: the defense of the revolution in Kingston and Fort Stanwix and Ticonderoga; the travels of Harriet Tubman, crossing the Hudson, to and fro, to meet with the abolitionists in Boston, with John Brown down from Lake Placid, with Gerritt Smith and others; the voice of Franklin Roosevelt, carried along from New Hyde Park, his place of childhood, of manhood, of debility, and of courageous physical renewal; and just a little bit east, in the White Mountains, the voice of our one poet, Robert Frost, who asks of us a certain height. These various river crossings carry a hint of liberty, a whisper of freedom, a twilight afterglow of the set free gospel which our passages today acclaim.

HUDSON MOSES

I pity those who cannot overhear, when the need arise, the steadying confidence of a physically broken, spiritually muscular, Albany formed governor, who became President in the afterwash of the various floods of the 1920's. How much of Roosevelt's empathy was forged in his polio? How much of that abiding concern for the least, the last and the lost came directly out of personal faith wrought in personal experience? And how much do we miss when we think that the divine can use only our wellness and not our brokenness? At the start of the New Deal: *The test of our progress is not whether we add more to the abundance of those who have much; it is whether we provide enough for those who have too little.* Would you not have liked to have been at Chautuaqua in the summer of 1936 to hear one sentence: *This generation of Americans has a rendevous with destiny.* Or his last, fourth inaugural: *We have learned that we cannot live alone at peace; our own well being is dependent on the well being of other nations. We have learned to be citizens of the world, members of the human community.* Or his first, in the depths of the depression: *The only thing we have to fear is fear itself.*

STRENGTH IN WEAKNESS

We have lived long enough at ease with the pervasive materialism of our culture. We have abided long enough the distinguishing sense of entitlement which is the hallmark of our county. We have long enough appeased the abject loneliness of exurban America. It is time to cross the river, to cross the Hudson, to cross over to a disciplined, fierce commitment to the truth of the gospel, the faith of the gospel, as Paul says today. We may feel beset, before and behind. A tragic war. A horrific flood. Four years of images, in memory, we still have trouble imagining. Gas at $3 gallon. But it was not the might of the straggling Israelites which bound them to Yahweh. The bread of heaven, the mysterious manna, was given daily to a broken, cantankerous, cautious, doubting, stumbling crew of people, like every generation, brand new to the challenges of freedom. Nor was the might of Paul of Tarsus which bound him to Christ Jesus. The grace of the gospel came daily to a broken, lisping, epileptic, cantankerous, cautious, stumbling, short, tentmaker. Why do we think that the divine has use only for our strength? I draw your scrutiny to this easy to miss locution, "the faith of the gospel," by which Paul addresses his Philippians. This is the lived truth by which the earliest Christians *and you today* find courage to cross over the rivers of life, from the Hudson to the Jordan. It is a faith and truth which occasions imprisonment, receives attack, and evokes opposition.

For many years our children's great grandmother resided in an Albany nursing home. Her condition and her nobility in those years are somehow easier now to appreciate, with the advantage of some age and some distance. Her concern always to present herself with dignity, no matter what opposition, lingers like a fragrance. Her tenacious affirmation of the faith of the gospel, over against much physical opposition, remains clear in the memory. The price of freedom is vigilance, eternal vigilance. True for the physical life, and truer still for the life of faith.

One day, following the morning service, we visited a similarly dear saint in her home. She had been in hospital that week, and sat recuperating in her parlor. Her family was with her. And she had a story to tell.

That Tuesday, she prepared to be taken, by ambulance, from one hospital to another, for a particular procedure. She is a fine, older Methodist lady, so she prepared herself with what dignity one can muster in a hospital bed, robed in a hospital gown, and alone in the corridor of life. A little makeup, a comb and brush, some careful adjustments of remaining raiment, glasses perched, smile shining.

She could see the elevator door open, and her stretcher moving out. Then the attendants clearly mentioned her name as they signed the paper work at the desk. The nurse motioned across the hall in the general direction of her room. She poised herself, prepared to be a good, courteous patient. Down the hall the men came, and she waved. They returned the gesture. To her door they rolled—and then, remarkably, rolled on by! They passed to the next room, one inhabited alone by a frail, kindly woman who is deaf as a post. "Mrs. Smith?" "Yes," she replied, her volume in inverse proportion to her accuracy. Into the stretcher went the wrong woman, and down the hall they moved. My dear parishioner called out, used her buzzer, flailed her arms like a gypsy at the campfire. But in a New York minute they were gone, carrying away the wrong person. On the way home, following the procedure, someone apparently had the presence of mind to look at the stretchered woman's wrist band, name tag. I wonder how the reader felt not to see the name Smith. A rare moment of revelation.

In this case, little lasting harm occurred. Our hospitals, in fact, to my eye, given their hourly commitment to excellence and attention to detail, put other institutions to shame. We all know the fear of the wrong arm amputated, the wrong knee replaced, the wrong woman put in the stretcher. Physician's malpractice. But the news, good news, of medical malpractice is that you know soon—an hour, a day, a decade—what has happened, and you can endure it or correct it. So it goes with the physician's malpractice.

Not so with the metaphysician's.

Biological error lasts, at most, a lifetime. Theological error resides for three generations, or more. If, as ML King Sr. said, 'it takes three generations to make a preacher,' then it also takes three generations, or more, to recognize and correct the effects of metaphysical malpractice. You cannot fully see its effect for 20 or 40 or 60 or 80 years. And it is a short way from birdie to bogie, from clean cuts to nicks and scratches in innocent organs, mistaken severations and amputations, blood spilled and shed in the wrong bed. Choose the physical mistakes, for the metaphysical are so much more insidious, more damaging, more real.

CROSSING THE HUDSON

Representation is good, Redemption is great

We risk harm when we replace *redemption* with *representation*. Remember, friends, you are listening to a liberal of the liberals. But when we let the very worthy interests in representation eclipse the main work of the gospel, in redemption, we are making a surgical mistake. Direction, selection, election–shaping the future on the basis of representation, rather than redemption will not work, in the long run. Let us have Asian Americans, Native Americans, Latino Americans, African Americans, women, gays, tall, short, and otherwise multiplicitous leaders. But let us not elect them on that basis, mainly or only. Let us learn from our experience. Can they preach? Have they done so? Is there fruit? Do they have experience, proven not just promised? If not, we fail them, we fail ourselves, we fail our God. We need to cross the river from representation to redemption!

Incantation is good, Incarnation is great

We risk harm when we replace *incarnation* with *incantation*. The gospel of John affirms the incarnation of the Christ, in the flesh. That is—children's flesh, adolescent's flesh, young couples' flesh, people, people, people. The image of God. We have forsaken our passionate interest in people, young or old, fat or thin. Half our membership in the Northeast has been erased, since my ordination. Cataclysm. Apocalypse. A moment, maybe this one, when you look down at the stretcher and you see that the nametag is not what you expected. And you face failure. Face it. It won't kill you. Denying it will kill more than facing it. We have decided to enjoy incantation, instead, the pseudo worship that has eviscerated many of our churches across the region. We, for the most part, have not wanted to do the hard work of preaching and liturgical preparation. We prefer easy incantation to the rich announcement of incarnation. People notice. We need to cross the river from incantation to incarnation!

Innocence is good, Integrity is great

We risk harm when we replace *integrity* with *innocence*. Innocence is not holiness, nor holiness innocence. While there are many facets to this single haphazard metamedical blunder, the matter of sex alone should make it clear. In our region we no longer talk about sex—a tragic silence given the unfiltered filth of the internet that has invaded most homes far beyond our poor power to add or detract. After the flames of the 60's Jack Tuell and a couple of other Bishops sat over coffee and came up with the phrase, "in singleness celibacy, in marriage fidelity." Given the chaos of the time, the phrase made some ordering sense. But today it has served to muzzle and muffle fully honest talk about sex. Tuell's own confessional, repositioning sermon on homosexuality specifically mentions, and laments, the phrase. But the gays are the least of our problems. Our malpractice has caused fairly good people to mask their struggle for integrity, in failure as well as success, with a false innocence, assuming there can be no integrity without innocence. Our own area has had past denominational leadership that was struggling with personal identity and sexual expression. Is there any wonder that we have no significant conference or area work on human sexuality? We need to find our voice again, to honor God's good gift of sexuality, and its best expression within the sacramental rite of marriage. We need to pull the scalpel out of the wrong intestine, and wash up and start again. We need a fuller conversation. You can have integrity and holiness without innocence. I might redact Tuell this way: *in singleness integrity; in partnership fidelity.* We are crossing a river from the east bank of innocence to the great capital region of integrity!

Independence is good, Interdependence is Great

We risk harm when we replace *just war* with just *war, interdependence* with *independence.* The 2003 invasion of Iraq jettisoned our inherited experience codified in just war theory. It was preemptive, unilateral, imperial, unforeseeable, post-Christian, immoral, and wrong. Anybody with half a Bible could see that. But what did our pulpits say in 2002 and 2003? With a baker's dozen exceptions, across the country, we said: *not sure, don't know, support the troops, what a world, hope it all works out, give it up to God . . .* We had the wrong woman in the stretcher all along, but we just were too busy tuning our electric guitars to see so. Now 1900 are dead in Iraq, and hundreds more in New Orleans. It took 25 years, but the chickens did come home to roost. Let us cross over the Hudson, from the quiet eastern shore of independence to the brightly lit capitol of interdependence!

Christology is good, Theology is great

We risk harm when we replace *God* with *Jesus*. I love Barth, too, but Jesus is not all the God there is. We are still wallowing, as Doug Hall warned a generation ago (you see it does take a long time), in a Unitarianism of the Second Person of the Trinity. Just when the gentle wisdom of Wilfred Cantwell Smith, Huston Smith and so many others might have broadened our creaky Christomonism, we let in the Calvinists. Yes, we want to name the name. The name that is above every name. But that name does not drown the others, like a Gulf hurricane, or bomb the others, like a Desert Storm, or burn the others like a terrorist hijacking. When John wrote "I am the way" he meant that wherever there is a way—there is the Christ, wherever there is truth—there is Christ, wherever there is life—there Christ is, too. The day I met the Clergy Session of Conference, at Syracuse University, to be passed on for orders, Huston Smith walked over to the session from his office on the other side of the quad. He stood by me, outside as I waited. I was nervous. He assured me I had no reason to be. We need that voice today! The mystery of God is greater than the measure of

Calvin's mind, and greater than the Christology of the Reformation, and greater than the purpose driven life. We are crossing over the raging river from exclusivity to particularity, from Christology to Theology!

Giving is good, Tithing is great

We risk harm when we replace *tithing* with *giving*. The Christian life involves specific, serious commitments with regard to time, to people, and to money. To be a Christian is to worship weekly, to keep faith in marriage and other close relationships, and to give away 10% of what one earns. Not more than 10% but not less either. Where did we go off the reservation here?

The pervasive materialism of our culture receives its rejection in tithing, not in mere giving. The enduring sense of entitlement in our county receives its contradiction in tithing, not in mere giving. The abject loneliness of exurban life receives its denial in tithing, not in mere giving. We have spent too much time trying to encourage people, bit by bit, to keep faith.

How would your spouse feel if you said, "You know, I was 40% faithful this year, a 5% increase from last year." That would not fly in my home. Other things would fly (pans, knives, etc.), but that would not! Nor can this euphemistic blather about "abundance," a culture of abundance, last much longer. We need full affirmation of a culture of scarcity, not abundance, and the virtues, once our stock in trade, that come with scarcity: frugality, saving, temperance, industry, and, yes, tithing. Let us cross over and rest in the shade of the tithing trees!

17

Utica

The Far Side of Fear

Philippians 1; Exodus 16

AN OPENING PRAYER

A͟L͟M͟I͟G͟H͟T͟Y͟ G͟O͟D͟, Y͟O͟U͟ P͟R͟O͟C͟L͟A͟I͟M͟ *your truth in every age by many voices: Direct, in our time, we pray, those who speak where many listen and write what many read; that they may do their part in making the heart of this people wise, its mind sound, and its will righteous; to the honor of Jesus Christ our Lord. Amen.*

DELIVERANCE TO THE CAPTIVES

We are delivered from captivity, from the power of fear, in the announcement of the Gospel. It is the word of faith that delivers from enslavement to fear. From separation anxiety, survival anxiety, performance anxiety, anxiety about anxiety. The good news carries us to the far side of fear.

You may another selection, but to my ear there is hardly another text in the Holy Scripture more badly understood, and rudely interpreted than Philippians 2. In our time, it has been falsely accused of triumphalism and falsely used for religious one-upmanship. It has been cited as the basis for a kind of non-Biblical evangelism that has no common ground with the passage itself. Its last hymnic lines curl repeatedly and tiresomely from the lips of television preachers, whose work would be the very last thing the passage, its author, or its audience would affirm. A word of liberation has become, in the common hearing, a word of enslavement, of the very kind addressed and attack in the verses! Most ironically, the text of Philippians 2, and its pearl of great price, the Christ hymn of verses 5–11, is often regarded as a staunchly conservative, traditional, utterly *biblical* poem, when in fact it is pure Gnosticism, wholly composed, in its original frame, in a non-christian setting, only to be borrowed and used here, by Paul, to communicate with his formerly pagan Gnostic and newly Christian Philippians.

Paul is alone in prison. His own missionary work, as we can overhear from chapter 1, is under revision and redirection by others who claim he has failed in certain key areas. His own personal future is more than cloudy, including the possibility of death, and again, his ruminations in the first chapter bear this out. He acclaims deliverance for the captives, you and me, a saving drumbeat along the Mohawk river of life. He has a sight line to the far side of fear.

One little word will suffice to illumine the rest. *Slave*. Here the NRSV has got it much righter than earlier translations. He became a slave. What does this mean? That Jesus was an indentured servant? Hardly. Paul knows little and says less about the earthly Jesus, other than that he died on a cross. He hardly has any interest in placing Jesus in the circle of actual slavery, common as it was in his day. What then? It is a puzzle, without the floodlight of our knowledge of the main competitor religion of the day, Gnosticism. For the Gnostics to be human is to be enslaved. Every human is a slave.

The Gnostics sang hymns, like that in the *Poimandres*. In these hymns they celebrated a great mind in the universe. They acclaimed the forms of God. They spoke of emptying and filling. They especially and repeatedly compared human life to enslavement in these writings and hymns. To be human is to be ensnared by the elemental spirits of the universe, to be at the mercy of the cosmic, that is historical and natural, forces all around us. To be human is to be humbled by death, even ignominious death. They sang the praise of a Redeemer, who was once preexistent in the form of God, who came to earth in human guise, and who returned to the father's house, preparing rooms for his followers, and being the most highly exalted. The name beyond all names, the light beyond all lights, before Whom all bow. Sound familiar?

Philippians 2 is a Gnostic hymn.

Paul has lifted and used it, because his hearers know it and because it suits his message. It is a plundering of the Egyptians, a use of the cultural language of the day to convey great tidings of good news. You need not fear. You need not fear. God has broken in upon our fear, and invaded this life with liberation to live fully and lastingly! God's beachhead is the cross. The cross is the presence of God in suffering. The cross is the love of God in suffering. The cross is the power of God in suffering, to free the slaves—every human being—from fear.

THE STOOPING CHRIST

I wonder if we can recapture, by the imagination, Paul's decision to recite for himself and for his correspondents, a hymn to the faithful love of God that carries us over, to the far side of fear. Here is the outspoken leader of a religious movement charged with atheism, with rejecting the gods of the empire. Here he is alone in prison. Here he affirms what can only be affirmed by faith, the victory of the visible over the invisible, of God beyond the many gods, of Christ the failed messiah over the cross of his failure. He does so in measured, nearly serene tones.

His attention is captured by the servant Christ, here so like the figure in Isaiah. To be a human being, for Paul, is to be a slave under the control of malignant powers, to live in a world in which the human being has fallen prey to powers that are aligned and arranged against what is truly human.

As one himself immersed in fear, Paul, seized by Christ, is set to singing in his prison cell. Maybe today, given our fears, we may hear something of his happy news.

TODAY'S ENSLAVEMENTS

Of course, we do not share Paul's worldview, nor that of his Gnostic hymn writer, from whom he lifted this passage. Nor that of the Philippians. We do not believe in elemental spirits, or the cosmic star journeys, or the natural enslavement which grounds Paul's thought, his worldview is not ours. *But his world is.* We live in the same world, and the Scripture, realer and harder than other writings, soberly so reminds us. We may not be

Gnostics, but we know the same fears and failures that they did, and that caused them to say and sing what they did.

We are a people drenched in fear. It has been coming for a decade, increment by increment, so that now, every single initiative, every move, every dream is soggy with dread. 1998: "I did not have sex with that woman . . ." and we begin to fear a famine of the word, a dearth of truth, and every public leader and statement falls under that fearful shadow. I preached in San Diego in 2000 and the woman in the pew with Jan said to her friend, "I wonder what his agenda is?" 1999: You have forgotten Y2K? We had a committee on it here. Will the ball fall on New Year's at all? 2000: a forever election, still not resolved in some minds, causing a fear that ripples still about the reliability of counters and machines and institutions and courts. 2001: 9/11, and the smoke is still swirling in our nostrils. 2002: the ramp up of the case, el Qaeda, WMD, testimony at the UN, a darkening horizon. 2003: war, begun, ended, and endless. 2004: an election decided by the state of Ohio, bitterly contested, making good friends think thrice about which issues they will mention. And 2005: the rain fell and the flood came and the wind blew and beat upon the house divided against itself. Hurricane upon hurricane. Friends, that decade long cascade of fear is the best illustration I can give you of what the ancients meant by the enslavement of the human condition, the cosmic powers, the elemental spirits of the universe. They cause fear.

THINGS FALL APART

From the days of Natie Bumpo to the hoola hoop, Utica succeeded. Nestled along the lovely Mohawk River, in some clear day view of the Adirondack foothills, this settled combination of waves of immigrants has had a storied history. Its older sections and neighborhoods still adorn and beautify like Cana of Galilee. Today, however, one would not necessarily point to Utica as a great shining city on a hill. It feels like a town whose best days are past. The older I get, the better I was, saith the preacher. It feels like a fear of the future has bought property in Utica, controlled the means of production there, been elected to school boards and hospital corporations, infiltrated the fire and police departments, been elected to high office, and generally set the rhythm, tone and beat in this once fair city. It would be nice to think that the dynamics there are unique to the state of New York.

We are within earshot of another word, another way of being. My teacher put it this way: *"Paul conceives of sin as a power, not as defilement or guilt. In the thoroughly real event of Christ's crucifixion, God's war of liberation was commenced and decisively settled, making the cross the foundation for Paul's apocalyptic theology . . . God has done it! . . . You are to live it out! . . . You are to live it out because God has done it and will do it . . ."*[1] We truly can live it out, over against all the freeze tag fears that keep us in distress. Christ is with us! In Spirit! And Truth! In kindness, in community, in dreams, in ingenuity, in hope.

BLESSED

Kindness helps us find the far side of fear.

My friend took his own rascally dog, Spot, to the veterinarian, and sat, among a dozen humans and another dozen canines in the waiting room. Spot was in like a shot and out like a shot, and howled like the hound he is. But as Spot and his weary owner were bidding the vet farewell, they saw a strange moment of blessing.

Up toward the examination room walked a nine year old girl, holding, like a temple offering, a motionless mound underneath a blanket. She walked to the doctor. She stopped. She slid the blanket aside to show a motionless, just breathing pet, utterly American, of 15 different blood lines. A mongrel, but her mongrel. The dog looked about 400 years old, ears drooping, tongue lax, eyes glazed, resting in some young but familiar arms. The looked at each other, the young woman and the old doctor. A long field of silence spread out between them, and gradually engulfed the whole waiting room. And her pleading eyes said, "Can you help?" And his weathered eyes said, with the reluctance of the heart, "I truly wish I could." Then her eyes began to fill and to say all that we really cannot say without the laughter of love and the tears of tenderness. His eyes bowed a little to show respect, to honor. She found somewhere the strength to lift up the old pooch, up to where the doctor's arms could enfold the dog. And he stooped down, down far enough to where he could take the blanket and all its precious treasure. He whispered to her ear, lightly touched her head, bestowing a hug and a kiss and what may have been her first real blessing, which was all that kept her solvent as she tumbled, headlong and

---

1. J. L. Martyn, *Anchor Bible: Galatians* (New York: Doubleday), 221.

convulsed, through the outer door. Those who can touch us at the hour of death do offer such a blessing.

A COMMUNITY OF HELPERS

Others help us find the far side of fear.

The Oneida parsonage is an ante-bellum main street battleship with 2 living rooms, 3 floors, 5 bedrooms, 2 studies, and, best of all, balloon ceilings punctured at various places by preachers' kids over the decades. Across the street is an acre lawn, which at age 13, and for a set price, I agreed to rake. The autumn days went by. Other things interfered. It rained a lot that fall. I sat watching the rain, under the balloon ceilings, knowing that once the snow came it would be too late. I feared that, and gripped by that fear I failed. I just never quite got at it, at the right time, and winter came, and failure and shame. Imagine the relief when, in the springtime, others and family and friends and church helped move the snow sodden leaves. I had to ask. But asked, they helped.

DREAMS THAT REVEAL

Dreams help us find the far side of fear.

This summer, after some days to rest, and once I could sleep through the night, to 6am not 4am, I had this dream. It was set in the Oneida parsonage living room, whose balloon ceilings carried the tell tale marks of childhoods past. Two of the most Christian women I have known sat beside me, in the dream, one from Syracuse and one from Rochester. They have never met but they share loyalty, love, fidelity, good humor, widowhood and some age. It is 6am and I wake up screaming at them, "I cannot do a week's work for a day's pay." I shout it rudely and twice. Then I wake up.

Here is our fearful dilemma, which a now and then dream does reveal. You cannot sustain the ministry of the church for 10cents on the dollar, or one penny for seven. Dreams identify problems that then can be solved (a problem identified is a problem solved), and so show us the far side of fear.

A LITTLE INGENUITY

Ingenuity helps us find the far side of fear.

Utica does evoke the fear of failure. Twenty years ago, though, long before the book *Who Moved My Cheese*, some Utican decided to fly a kite, to try something. He took the empty factories, and open streets, and remaining vacant parks, and civic need and added . . . sneakers and ingenuity. He created *The Boilermaker*, the world's largest 15k footrace, which draws 12,000 participants a year, and ends with a Sunday morning celebration that includes nourishment, rock and roll, prizes, oranges, jet planes, fireworks, pins and mugs and hugs, all out behind the old Utica Boiler Factories. Rather than seeing only what was wrong, he bought some sneakers, took lemons, and made lemonade. And some other beverages. Monet was asked once what he added to his paints and oils to make such colorful beautiful portraits: "brains" he replied. A little ingenuity will carry us to the farther side of fear.

YORK

Historical perspective helps us find the far side of fear. As Wesley said, the clergy are meant to represent the unity and continuity of the church through the ages.

The cathedral in York, we felt, evoked the beauty of this Asbury First sanctuary. Certainly it carries more age, more expanse, more detailed artistry than our own dear church, and yet it still carries that spiritual resemblance that we do sense in one place for another. So we might want to listen to a York voice for a New York minute. Practicing Christians and vibrant congregations are increasingly rare in Europe. A York minister, a priest in the Church of England, was confronted recently with this stark reality. Membership in decline, buildings in disrepair, programs in disarray.

The question he was asked might have been one I could have written: "the church is dying, and what shall we do when it is gone".

Oh, he said, unflappable, "Well, yes, that might could happen, given, you know, the currents of the times, and the, shall we say, less than spirited energy of our people for things other than the material, yes, my good fellow, it could so do."

"Whatever then will you do?"

"Oh, I suppose then, why we will find a table, a loaf, and carafe of wine, and we will start all over."

There is the persistence of faithful leadership. There is the process of faithful leadership. There is the purpose of faithful leadership.

Therefore, work out your own salvation in fear and trembling, for it is God who is at work in you, enabling you both to will and to work for God's good pleasure.

Pastoral Prayer:

Gracious and Holy God, You who has enfolded us with Your Spirit, we are grateful that You created us free and curious persons, inhabitants of this beautiful earth. You have revealed Your love for us by giving us the capacity to make choices, the ability to heed Your guidance, and the constancy of Your Presence that can still our fears. We lay before You our prayers for our city, for our nation, for our world all with its sores and wounds, its soldiers that fight for freedom's sake, its fears and frustrations, its ideals and its injustices, its affluence and its agony. Make us quiet before its needs that we may be moved by Your Spirit to respond from our hearts. We come in faith with even our most personal petitions; so we pray: let our love for one another be warm and tender and our compassion responsive and deep. Hear our soft tears when we weep for loneliness or out of fear; inspire us to pray and to respond to those left homeless and ever fearful because of storm upon storm; extend Your cool hand to quiet us when anger is a feverish illness; watch with us in our hour of death; bless the grieving with the comfort that every grief is known in Christ's heart and safely shared in the company of Christ's people. Change us O God from a fearful people to Your confident people, from closed to open, from shaken to courageous, that we might risk the work of establishing peace, justice and equality, right here, over there, everywhere. Grant us all some new hope and reassurance because we have been together to sing Your Praises, to hear Your Word, and to be strengthened once more to seek Your Will and to walk in Your way. We know that in all things You work to bring forth whatever may be good. Therefore, we open our lives to You with the yearning prayer of generations Come Holy Spirit, Come. Grant us Thy peace. Amen.

18

Ithaca

After the Fall

Exodus 32:1–14; Philippians 3:4–14

ITHACA'S FALLS

Failure is a part of life. If you play, you will lose. If you bat, you will strike out. If you keep your clubs and use them, you will put a ball into the sand trap. If you participate in life, you are surely going to fail . . . That anniversary date just slipped your mind . . . oops . . . Your husband's birthday—that was last week . . . oops . . .

The rightwising of faith, of which Paul speaks today, brings the power to face failure: to admit it, assess it, and accept it, and then live with it. The question is not whether we will fall. We will. Trip, stumble, and fall—the fate of one and all. The question is how we live *after the fall*.

Like the cascading falls in Ithaca, beautiful they are, Taughannock, Treman, Buttermilk, and like the descending poetry of Ecclesiastes, soaring it is, life keeps the evening and the rain before us. "Evening"—such a multilayered, meaningful word. The Psalms and their cadence of movement from lament to thanksgiving do as well.

I missed the chance to cause our children to memorize Ecclesiastes. Pity. It is worth remembering that . . . .*all the rivers run to the sea . . . the sun also rises . . . in much knowledge is much sorrow . . . better is the beginning than the ending . . . do you see something that is new? It has been before . . . vanity, vanity, all is vanity . . . what gain has the worker from his toil? . . . the race is not always to the swift . . . time and chance happen to all.*[1]

ADMIT IT

We have a harder time speaking about failure than we do about money or sexuality. Yet failure is a part of life, like sunset and rain. We should be quite doubtful that we necessarily know, by the way, when we have failed. Unamuno wrote so long ago: "Truly I tell you, you do not know when you have succeeded." Or failed, for that matter, we could add. Failure is something about which we all have direct knowledge.

It might make our children more open to their own true selves and actual experience, if we did not always expect that they be practically perfect in every way. They are human beings, not human doings, human beings, not divine. To err is human. To fail is too.

One of our less loquacious children decided, some years ago, to enroll in a high school photography course, on the mistaken information that it was an easy A. This misinformation, it happened, was powerfully mistaken in every direction. The teacher was a Prussian martinet, demanding to the nth degree. The syllabus had Latin subheadings. The reading list went nine pages. The papers were two a week and the projects two a month. There was no mercy, no forgiveness, nor grace. Only sweat, blood, and, subsequently, some tears.

Of course we knew none of this at the time. "How is your photography course?" O, fine. Good. Really. The teacher neglected to submit a midcourse grade. So, we just asked again. O, fine. Good. Really. Then the report card came, as it does, like autumn, like the stewardship appeal, like age itself. Relentless. And guess what. We had the experience of seeing the 6th letter of the English alphabet affixed under the name of one of our children. His first non A or B.

I was my usual, calm, phlegmatic self. *F! How Can You Get An F! We Don't Get F/s In This Family! How Could This Happen! What Were You Thinking! This Is Rochester, You Can't Fail Photography Here! It's*

---

1. Ecclesiastes 1:7, 5, 18; 7:8; 1:10, 2; 3:9; 9:11.

Like Failing Baseball In Cooperstown, Basketball In Springfield, Boxing In Canastota, Football In Canton, Physics At Los Alamos, Wind Studies In Chicago, Surfing In Malibu, Theology In Tubingen, Religion At the Vatican, Skiing In The Vail, Politics In Washington . . . (you begin to get the idea).

This helpful parental counsel was less than cheerfully received. As it turned out, the poor kid did have reasons not entirely of his own causation. We negotiated and moved on. But it might have been better for all involved, if the good news of the Christ who lives past failure had been more centrally on our minds. We all fail. Failure is embedded in life. If you choose to play, you will lose some. If you swing the bat at all, you will strike out. If you pay the greens fees, someday you will put one in the sand. If you decide to participate, you will fail at some point. You can bank on it.

And while our dear child may have failed, we also could truly see that we too had failed him, as had others. In hindsight. Failure, like success, is a team sport. It takes a village—to fail.

ASSESS IT

One great advantage of failure admitted, is that once admitted it can teach us. We learn most from our failures.

Groups help us find the far side of failure.

We have a hard time admitting failure. Men in particular so struggle. We are quiet about our hurts.

After men's group one morning a fine soul stepped over to me and said "Bob . . . your car . . . the Sebring . . . uh . . . did it . . . I mean did it, uh, die? . . ."

"Yah" I said . . . "jeez" he said . . . "Yah" I said . . .

It helps to have a small group with whom to share and consider loss, disappointment, failure. We love to succeed and we are in a success culture.

Yet our best moral exertions can, like over exercise, cause injuries, if our very noble and well-chosen interest in success makes us fear, and fear failure, which is inevitable to some degree in every life.

Nothing succeeds like success.
If at first you do not succeed, try and try again.
Come back with your shield or on it.
Winning isn't everything, it's the only thing.

Work conquers all.
I can do all things through Christ who strengthens me.
I think I can, I think I can, I think I can . . .

But some measure of failure touches every one of us. And we learn some lessons:

You will fail.
It will not kill you.
It will hurt, bad.
You may learn from it.
It may help to talk about it.

ACCEPT IT

The grace of failure admitted and assessed is the power to accept the past and move on. In a way, this is all that Paul is saying in Philippians 3. What he thought was success was not. What he thought of as worthless was priceless. What he once valued has been discarded. He now can rely on the health that comes from the faith of Christ. He has been set right. We may live on the basis not of what we have achieved but what we have received, not on the basis of what we have done but what God has done, not on the currency of religion but on the down payment of the spirit in faith.

Many of Flannery O'Connor's stories make this strong point.

In similar fashion, this great church stands, daily, as a powerful influence upon women and men who want to admit, assess, and especially accept failure. One comes after years of mixed experience, to return to the pew of this strong church, and to be strengthened by your strength. Another comes at the end of life, to sit in worship underneath the great pillars of the church, and to be strengthened by your strength. Another comes after abject failure, to be take a photograph in front of the great spire of the church, to be strengthened by your strength.

As your nave is like that of Yorkminster, your spirit is that of the York Anglican priest who, when asked what he would do if all the people finally left and the church collapsed, said, "Well, we would get a table and a loaf of bread and a chalice of wine and start all over again."

That is the power that Christ gives, to live by faith, after the fall. It is the acceptance that allowed Paul, and allows us, to sing, *this one thing I do, forgetting what lies behind, and straining forward to what lies ahead, I press on toward the prize of the upward call of God in Christ Jesus my Lord.*

19

Lake Placid

A Survey of Freedom

Philippians 4

GREETING

Travel for a moment to Lake Placid. Take the trail up along the ridge of Whiteface Mountain (5000ft). Stop for an autumn moment, in the sun. East, West, South, and especially due North, here is a natural survey of mountainous freedom, symbolic of the Bible—its main theme freedom, and its four compass points of faith, fact, fairness, and future. The Bible is a book about freedom.

Life does not lack for holiness, but only for a sense of the holy. We today place in our children's hands the gift of Holy Scripture, in an hour to worship the Holy God, in a space and place devoted to what is highest and holiest in life. So Paul can call his Philippians those "whom I love and long for."

These moments matter. It matters how many children are baptized each year, and more, how many others could have been. It matters how many youth are confirmed each year, and even more, how many others could have been. It matters how many receive the sacrament of Holy Communion, season by season, and still more, how many others could have done. It matters how many sentient women and men hear the Good News preached on Sunday morning, and still more, how many others could have done. These things matter.

It truly matters how many of our boys and girls in Rochester are handed a Bible, and so given that priceless perspective, that eternal excitement, that reliable reservoir of the Word of God. God is loving us into love and freeing us into freedom. The pulpit is freedom's voice. The church is freedom's defense. And the Bible is freedom's book. The Bible is a survey of freedom.

Now there are other ways in which to survey the strange landscape of the Holy Scripture. What James Smart decried a generation ago, "The Strange Silence of the Scripture in the Churches", is true of you as well. All books suffer in a video culture, including the Good Book. You may yourself continue as literate (not one who can read only but one who does), but your grandchildren are stumbling about in other thickets. So if the content of the Bible is ever stranger and more foreign in an increasingly illiterate (not those who cannot read but those who do not) culture, then how much greater is the lack of capacity to interpret the book whose contents themselves are distant relations.

The old levees of biblical understanding have given way to the great flood of video culture, whose hurricane forces have carried in the disease of Biblicism, the destruction of literalism, the rampant looting of Providentialism, the tidal crash of unbiblical bibliolatry. These levees cannot be rebuilt in a New York minute. They have to be painstakingly renewed, Bible Sunday by Bible Sunday, church school by church school, campground by campground, Disciple class by Disciple class, and sermon by sermon. We are doing some of this today. We are placing a library of liberty into the hands of another generation. We did so 15 years ago, right here, in this same sanctuary. One of those boys is in Iraq this morning. One of those girls is practicing medicine today. One of those boys is in missions today. One of those girls has her own girls today. With them, either in fact or in memory, goes the Holy Scripture. What kind of book have we given them? In what key is the music of scripture best played? What is the Bible about? From what angle of vision do we best see the Bible?

FAITH

Turn East. We see the Bible with the eyes of faith. Faith comes by hearing and hearing by the word of God. The righteousness of God is from faith to faith. Abraham had faith and it was reckoned to him as righteousness. Yes, we may affirm, the Bible is a survey of faith. Faith is trusting reliance upon God. Says Huston Smith: "we are in good hands and in recognition of that fact it behooves us to bear one another's burdens." You are committed, as Methodists, to a combination of a deep personal faith and an active social involvement. Holiness, personal and social. Ruth had faith to leave. Esther had faith to speak. Eudora and Synteche had faith to work. Faith is the courage to shake off sleep and worry and get to church on Sunday. Faith is the courage to tote up one's income and give away 10%. Faith is the courage to keep faith with one's partners, through thick and thin. Faith is a personal commitment to an unverifiable truth. Yes, the Bible is about faith. We give our children the grammar of faith, the language of faith, the mother tongue of faith, when we give them their Bibles. Whether or not they choose to speak is their decision. Here is Paul's testimony of this faith: "Do not be anxious about anything but in all things by prayer and supplication with thanksgiving let your requests be made known to God."

For 2000 years women and men have found faith in the hearing of the Scripture. These are the stories and events that give us the courage to face death with dignity, disappointment with honesty, and failure with a steady hope. In the apocalyptic language of the New Testament, this faith is revealed to us. It comes by inspiration, imagination, invocation. Faith is being grasped, being seized by a love that will not let go. As Karl Barth said, visiting New York City, and asked to state his faith: "Jesus loves me this I know, for the Bible tells me so."

But faith alone, with due respect and apologies to Luther, is not the whole story. In fact, such a reading of the Bible can become the Bible's undoing. The Bible is not to be memorized, but interpreted. It is not meant only to be repeated, but to be read. It opens its pages best not to faith alone but to faith seeking understanding. In our tradition, the Bible is not the only source of truth, primary though it be. There are many places where the Bible may be theologically though not historically accurate, which leads to another thought.

FACT

Look South. We understand the Bible with the mind of reason. The Bible is, second, a book of fact. For more than 200 years, generations of scholars have critically studied the 66 books of the Bible. We have learned a great deal about its languages, history, geography. We have seen the four different hands at work in the writing of the books of Moses. The Greek influences on Ecclesiastes we now appreciate. Isaiah's three different modes we comprehend. Jesus meets us in these wondrous pages, and the few facts of his life of which we are certain we can list, as James Sanders did years ago. We know that Paul probably did not write 2 Thessalonians, any more than he wrote 3 Corinthians, a document from the third century. The Revelation to St John we now understand, if that is the right word, in the context of similar apocalypses from antiquity. The withering inspection and criticism of the Scripture since 1750 have borne fruit. Law, Prophets, Writings, Gospels, Letters, Apocalypse: all six parts of the Bible have factual features. We have searched the Scriptures for 200 years. Here Paul names names: two women, one man, many co-workers. Facts. Earliest Christians. Facts endure. Here Paul discloses his worldview: time is short, the end is near, the day is at hand, as Dave Brubek would put it: 'its later than you think.' Or, in verse: "The Lord is near." It is a fact that Paul's worldview is not our own. But his world is, and that too is a fact.

In fact, the factual limitations of the Scriptures have been the primary learning of the modern era. The world was not created in 7 days, unless by a day you mean 15 billion years. The human being was not made in a day, unless you mean by a day, the emergence out of primordial ooze that began 3 billion years ago, and is still continuing today. The words of Moses and of Jesus are not video recordings of speeches captured by unerring scribes, but are far more—words formed in the community of faith. Most famously, the scientific—religious showdown of the 20th century was captured early on in the Scopes trial of 1925. We remember or misremember the trial largely through the play *Inherit the Wind* which itself was more theologically than historically accurate. William Jennings Byrant was not the buffoon caricature of that fine play, nor was his enemy Darwinism as much as it was Social Darwinism, nor was the generally insipid cast of old time religion anything like accurate with regard to golden rule Christianity, then or now. Bryant is made to say, "I am more interested in the Rock of Ages than in the ages of rocks," and is pilloried by the protagonist, Clarence Darrow: "the Bible is a book, a good book, but not the only book." In the matter of fact, the Bible carries a more limited weight and role in our time.

But science, and its measured facts alone, can only carry a part of the sacred story. As Justice Holmes said, science gives major answers to minor questions, and religion gives minor answers to major questions. Science alone—as wonderful as it is—does not cross the bridge from fact to value, cannot swim the river from flesh to spirit, has not forded the creek from brain to mind, and cannot judge about the things that matter most—love, death, memory, hope, thought, desire, heaven and God. To the one most important question of life, God, science has no response. Because there is no conclusive evidence. But absence of evidence is not evidence of absence (H Smith).

FAIRNESS

Face West. We hear the Bible with the ears of fairness. The Bible is, third, a hymn to fairness. To justice, equality, the right and the good. In our time, African Americans and others have found again the liberating power of the Hebrew Scriptures, of Exodus and Amos. The suffering masses of Latin America and Asia have returned to, and been nourished by, the abiding picture of God in the Bible, God who has a preferential option for the poor. Most lastingly, the feminist movement has found in the pages of the patriarchal Bible, a warning about justice, justice delayed, and justice denied. The deep rivers of fairness and justice have been diverted to flow over the dry land of prejudice, injustice, and patriarchy. The Bible is a testament, on this view, to fairness. What does the Lord require of you but to do justice, love mercy, walk humbly with your God? It is easier for a camel to pass through the eye of a needle than for a rich man to enter the kingdom of God. So, the Bible is a resource for liberation movements of many and good kinds, and the record of the churches in peace and justice is improved. Here in Philippians Paul asks for unity and peace. For fairness. He exposes his reliance on the kindness of strangers and the company of women. Paul had great regard for his partners in the Gospel, Eudia and Syntyche, whatever he may have written elsewhere about liturgical proprieties. "I urge Euodaia and Syntyche to be of the same mind . . . help these women for they have struggled beside me in the work of the gospel." Beside. Not beneath. Not behind. Not before. Beside.

It is difficult to overestimate the crucial significance of this perspective on the Scripture. Real religion is never very far from fairness, from justice. Fairness does not always mean equality, nor justice always similarity. There are varieties of gifts. But the renderings of Moses, the citations of Micah, the meditations on Job, the pictures of Jesus, the readings of Paul and even the explorations of the Apocalypse which in our time have focused on fairness, and justice, have a penultimate power. "The moral arm of the universe is long, but it bends toward justice," said Martin Luther King. None of us fully ever deconstructs our own background, our own culture. We need, however, the whiter and maler especially that we are, to acknowledge our own privileges. The sense of limitation and injustice to which the Biblical measure of fairness responds is the gift of our time to the unforeseen future.

Still, fairness alone is not the full Bible.

Our children now see their Bibles, read with some understanding, and hear with concern. Bless their eyes and minds and hearts. Will they see the Bible in full through these lenses of faith, fact, and fairness? No, important and good as these views are, they are not the heart of the matter. They are not the heart of the Bible nor the heart of the church nor the heart of the matter. They are good, but not the final good. You will sense in them the predominant views of the Bible to date—pre-modern, modern, post-modern, or, traditional, scientific and liberal. Faith: the traditional view. Fact: the scientific view. Fairness: the liberal view. Let me show you a still more excellent way . . .

FUTURE

Head North. Follow the drinking gourd. The Bible is preeminently more than faith alone, fact preserved, or fairness defended. The Bible is a survey of freedom, divine and human. In a word, the Bible is a book about freedom. God's freeing love, and our freedom in love. God is loving us into love and freeing us into freedom. God's way with us is loving and free, free and loving. You cannot coerce another into freedom, and you cannot frighten another into love. But note this well: *this freedom is mostly known as hope—hope for this earth and hope for eternal life, the future of freedom promised today.*

Strangely, then, the Bible is fully and precisely the word we need in our emerging 21st century.

This is the heart of what Paul writes to the Philippians. Yes, with pre-modernity, his words celebrate faith. Yes, with modernity his words carry fact. Yes, with post-modernity, his words seek fairness. But if that is all you have heard, you have missed the marrow of his meaning. Paul is singing here a song of freedom. With the best insights in all of Scripture, these words of his carry us out into the open space of God's future. Rejoice always . . . no anxiety about anything . . . whatsoever things are true . . . the Lord is near . . . Here is the radiance of resurrection, the freedom for which Christ has set us free. To the word of faith, Paul will say, yes, but work out your own salvation in fear and trembling. To the word of fact Paul will say, yes, but who hopes for what he sees? To the word of fairness, Paul will say, yes, but I know how to be abased and how to abound. The Bible is more than a source of inspiration, or of information or of insurrection. It is all those. But it is more. It is hope for the future! It is a survey of freedom, real freedom, the freedom from love and the freedom to love. The future holds an indestructible promise of freedom—of peace and joy in this life and of everlasting peace and joy in the life to come.

The Bible has the shocking temerity to recall for us our utter dependence on God and one another, our utter similarity before the cross, before death, before God. Personal faith, yes. Factual understanding, yes. The struggle for fairness, yes. But there is more. Our age has the chance to interpret the Bible in full, as a survey of freedom, divine and human. It is this shared gift of freedom that will deliver us from the evil of this age. We are free, and in the hands of the God of freedom. All of us. The same. In our time, we need, desperately need, to reclaim our religious commonality. Across this small planet, we are all more alike than we are different. And spare us, please, as Freud said, "the petty narcissism of small differences".

We all survive the birth canal, and so have a native survivors' guilt. All six billion.

We all need daily two things, bread and a name. (One does not live by bread alone). All six billion.

We all grow to a point of separation, a leaving home, a second identity. All six billion.

We all love our families, love our children, love our homes, love our grandchildren. All six billion.

We all age, and after forty, its maintenance, maintenance, maintenance. All six billion.

We all shuffle off this mortal coil en route to that undiscovered country from whose bourn no traveler returns. All six billion.

Ringing out—it is unmistakable in this text and on this morning and within this sanctuary—from the heart of the Bible is a transcendent hope of a future freedom, on earth as it is in heaven, but not for all that lacking in heaven. The transcendent beauty of this nave, the transcendent glory of this sanctuary, the transcendent loveliness of this music, the transcendent history of this congregation, the transcendent height of pulpit and depth of prayer here, hold a future freedom that will endure well beyond the days that all the bongo drums are in garage sales, and all the horizontal worship spaces have been reconverted to Walmarts.

This hope is for earth and for heaven. For a day when the lion will lay down with the lamb, and lamb will be able to sleep. Asbury First, this year, in a time of change, we truly need the Bible's perspective, its survey of freedom. We need its steady affirmation of faith, to steady us when we are anxious. We need its craggy collections of facts, when we might be tempted to avoid the harder facts. We need its preference for fairness, when we might be happier to take an easier, less just route. It will take faith, fact, fairness and more for us to prevail in this year. *And more.* We have no words really with which to name this. But the survey of freedom that is the Bible rests on resurrection. On a reliable future. In the resurrection they neither give nor receive in marriage, but they are like angels in heaven . . .

Not so long ago, we gathered in radiant laughter and heartfelt tears, to sing farewell to our friend. Here is what we sang. I heard the organ play it. I heard you sing it. And I saw the courage and confidence with which you did so:

> *And thou our sister gentle death*
> *Waiting to hush our latest breath*
> *Alleluia! Alleluia!*
> *Thou leadest home the child of God*
> *And Christ our Lord the way has trod*
> *O praise ye*
> *O praise ye*
> *Alleluia! Alleluia! Alleluia!*

Howard Thurman could have spent his whole ministry absorbed in the inherited expressions of faith. He chose to move forward instead. He could have spent his whole ministry engaged in the science of history and psychology. He looked farther out. He could have spent his whole ministry upon the vital issue of racial justice. He saw a farther horizon. He saw, knew, felt, and heard the Bible as a survey of freedom. One night he spent walking the beach, wading in the surf, and listening to the stars above in a cloudless canopy. He wrote, "The ocean and the night together surrounded my little life with a reassurance that could not be affronted by the behavior of human beings," wrote Thurman. "The ocean at night gave me a sense of timelessness, of existing beyond the reach of the ebb and flow of circumstances. Death would be a minor thing, I felt, in the sweep of that natural embrace."[1]

---

1. Howard Thurman, *With Head and Heart* (New York: Harcourt, 1979), 204.

20

Syracuse

A Wind at Midnight

Philippians 4:10-20

INTRODUCTION

Help me greet 4 visitors to our service who have in common an encounter with the wind at midnight. They share an experience of love, a special providence, the late gift of the spirit. It is no bad thing if one represents scripture, and another tradition, and a third reason, and a fourth experience. Because the gospel today challenges you to ponder whether you have had, or will have, such an encounter yourself with the mighty wind that blows sometimes even at midnight. Have you? *Is there any longer any meaning to the notion of a 'special providence,' a wind at midnight?*

SCRIPTURE

Here is Paul of Tarsus as he is writing to the Philippians. The 27 books of the New Testament all are written in Greek. They are written largely by gentiles to gentiles; though with care we can find Jewish background here and there. Except for those letters of Paul—which were written by the apostles to the gentiles! He is speaking very much as a Greek to a Greek in the last of part of one of his latest letters. Here at the very end, at last. Philippians he writes probably in Rome, probably in prison in Rome toward the end of his earthly ministry and he saves the best for last. You have heard him these weeks in the fall as we have traversed the Empire State together in earshot of his voice. And here he has celebrated the gift of God. He has applauded faith. He has honored Christ. He dodges. He means it full well here too. Christ is the end of religion and the beginning of faith working through love.

He rejoices with these his compatriots. This is his happiest and in many ways his most personal letter. Especially at the very end where he leaves behind doctrine, teaching and theology and he gets real personal.

He has received a gift and he is thrilled. You can feel it. He doesn't quite want to say it. He says, "I recognize that at last," and there is a key prepositional phrase in this passage, "at last you have revived your concern for me." Do you hear that celebrates a gift, hoping for a gift that doesn't come? And then it comes. And he says, "at last." And isn't this typical, just like a man who is afraid to admit his emotions, he goes on for the rest of the chapter to avoid what he is just about to say. He dodges. He fences. He parries. Oh he says, ". . . not that you really were trying to forget me. I know that you didn't have opportunity to send it." Yeah, right, sure Paul. Or, "No," he says "not that I needed it." "I didn't need it, no I didn't need it." "I know how to be abased and how to abound to be in plenty and in want, have much and to have little. Now I can do all things through him who strengthens me."[1] And later on, "No I didn't seek the gift. I sought the fruit of it that might go to your credit."[2] But though he shies away you feel it and you know the feeling. You've waited and waited and there it is and here it comes. And Paul receives and he fumbles faultingly around naming an experience of love. What later Wesley would call a special providence. And he challenges us: can you name and narrate such an episode in your spiritual journey. When the wind blows at midnight. *That's the thing about the wind: it's outside of our control but not outside of our experience.* Here is Paul standing in scripture.

TRADITION

Here is Rosa Parks, whose life we have celebrated this past week. "How does it happen that one finds the courage to do anything?" "I got on the

---

1. Philippians 4:11–13.
2. Philippians 4:17.

bus to go home." She may have grown up as we did with that old spiritual—*Oh won't you sit down, no I can't sit down, or won't you sit down, no I can't sit down, won't you sit down, no I can't sit down, I just got to heaven got to look around.* But here Rosa Parks sits and in that apocalypse, that moment of revelation, is born a new movement. A 318 day bus boycott in the range of reality of interposition and nullification. The States rights Alabama of the mid 1950's. And there she sits and with her we too. How does it happen? Aristotle says, "A good thing is the right thing at the right time in the right way." How do we know that nudge?

Can you name and narrate such a moment in your life? Her story resonates with us because it's part of our tradition. She was a Methodist. A life long African Methodist Episcopal. But more than that she grew up as you did in ear shot of a tradition that celebrates a wind at midnight. That recognizes that the wind can blow even in the ninth inning, in the fifteenth round, at the eleventh hour when it looks like it's almost too late.

That's what happened to Sara. Sara was old, she was really old. Our children grew up in a neighborhood in which they shared "Your momma" stories. While most of them can't be told here, one does comes to mind. "Your momma is so old that she waited table at the Last Supper." Sara is even older than that and yet she gives birth to a child. That's a tradition of the wind blowing at midnight. There's Rachel who's messed with by her older sister, Leah, who comes and takes Jacob away from her for seven years. And then at the late night hour he walks the lonely road home seven years later and finds his way at long last, like Odysseus returning home. And there finds himself and her real self. And without them we would not have had Joseph or Benjamin or the story of Genesis or the full sense of God's providence that also has a special particular dimension. There's Ruth who has to decide between leaving and living or staying and stagnating and she says, "Wither thou goest I will go."[3]

In just a few weeks in this beautiful nave we will sing the songs of Advent and Christmas including the hymn "Late in time behold Him come." There is Elizabeth and there is Mary and they each have a son, John and Jesus, conversing one to another from the womb. There is a wind blowing at midnight.

John Wesley was thrown from the second floor of his Dad's parsonage as it was burned by irate parishioners. And at age eight he knew that

---

3. Ruth 1:16

he was in the words of Habakkuk, "A brand plucked from the burning." Yours is a tradition that honors this pulsing presence hard to name. Not reducible finally to the reason.

Timothy Tyson has written a book *Blood Done Sign My Name* in which he remembers the adventures of his beleaguered itinerant preacher Dad in the Carolina's of the fifties and sixties. His Dad was a beleaguered integrationist at a time before that had become the popular view. And so he was moved every three years from one church to another. The first year you can't do anything wrong and the second year you can't do anything right and the third year either they leave or you leave. Well he was the one leaving most third years.

And then late at night the author remembers that one night as they were about to leave there was a scrabble sound at the back door and a knocking, no light, and a knock and a knock. And a voice says, "Reverend, Reverend you know I wanted you to hear this. I did hear what you said and I know you're right and I just want to tell you I'm so proud that you are my pastor" and off she went. There is a wind that sometimes comes right at the end.

This week someone, a neighbor perhaps, dropped off clothes at the Storehouse and marveled at our building going forward and the progress and she said, "Well you must have had one big gift." And I said, "No this was really done by many hands, some moderate size gifts but to date no one single great gift." But then I couldn't resist saying, "But the night is young you never know." The wind is blowing even when it courses through at midnight. No we cannot ascribe to her Methodism all of Rosa Parks heroism. It's not only from Methodism that her courage did arise. It's not just because she was weaned and raised on the grace and freedom of John Wesley that she did what she did. It's not only that she did drink from the living water of this tradition you are happy to call your own. It's not just because she was a Methodist—*but it helped.* Here stands Rosa Parks, part of your tradition.

REASON

Greet now for a moment John Wesley who comes forward: he who struggled his whole ministry with this question of the wind at midnight, of blessing and providence and the balance between enlightenment and enthusiasm. Wesley had a high regard as we must also have for the reason.

It is the reason that keeps at bay those ghosts that Goya feared long ago when he painted his Sleep of Reason. When reason sleeps people get hurt, reminded Goya. John Wesley had a great and high view of reason. But he also had a sense that there is some of life that is not reducible to the reason. And so as David Hempton says in his beautiful new book about Methodism, *Empire of the Spirit,* Wesley kept his movement on the edge always between faith and credulity. That raw, religious experience where sometimes you get it wrong. And sometimes he did. At times, he trusted the wrong person, followed the wrong movement, supported the wrong event and he got burned. But he kept alive a reasonable approach in life as well to those moments of presence. He says in sermon 67, "…that if God's care envelops the whole world and all of creation, in a general sense, if that is we are in God's hands, then we might say today in those hands there probably will be some moments when we feel the fingertips as well." Carefully to balance, reasonably to assess. But to recognize that not all of life, and certainly not all of faith, is reducible to the reason.

And there stands Wesley, our hero of reason for the day, which leaves us just one more.

EXPERIENCE

This really could be you. It could be him. It could be her. Our fourth guest is Jan Pennock. She is the granddaughter of a Scottish coal miner and the daughter of a Methodist preacher of Welsh extraction. Jan had the misfortune to marry, as had her grandmother, and her mother and her daughter now, a Methodist itinerate preacher and travel along with him— that is with me. We want to be remembered as those who affirm that the wind can blow at the midnight hour.

Let us be very clear. We know in our experience something of tragedy. We do. We know about unfathomable hurt. We know about immeasurable heartache. We know about inexplicable loss and painful failure. To say it again, we know the experience of tragedy. *But the presence of tragedy does not mean the absence of blessing. The presence of confusion does not mean the absence of insight. The presence of uncertainty, so human, does not mean the absence of the confidence that is born of obedience, which is your faith, the faith of Jesus Christ.* We bear witness that the wind can blow at midnight even in the experience of the Christian church and even in the life of the ministry.

1979—Carrying illness and a child, we heard late at night in a phone call from a superintendent who said, "We understand you might be ready to take a church? We got one." "The treasurer has died and the preacher has run off and it's not much of a church. But it's in Ithaca." You come too. And the wind blew at midnight.

1981—Looking as we had, it had become difficult to go on for graduate study in Methodism at that time. They were shutting the doors. Foolish move. We had looked Northeast and South and there was a moment when we remembered Montreal and McGill and a great place accessible, affordable, international, excellent, biblical and the public library even had the brochure. Right at the end—a wind at midnight.

1984—Driving north across the tundra of route 11 it wasn't late at night but the wind sure was blowing. We thought of a church open in Syracuse that we knew well. There was a bishop with a listening ear and off we went happy in God. The wind blows sometimes right at the end.

1994—My Aunt Jane has lived in Rochester for 30 years. So at holiday time I had always told folks there was only one other church in the area that I would even want to or feel called to serve. I never named it and no one ever asked, but she knew. And I would ask her always at holiday time: "How are things as Asbury First? How are people feeling there? How are the clergy doing? How's their health?!?!" (You can get a sense of our banter).

Then one day there came an envelope that sat on our piano bench and it was from my Aunt. It was somewhere around Christmas of 1994 and it said, "Bob, I just heard through the grapevine that they are going to make some changes at Asbury First." But at the same time the Bishop came and asked us to be a district superintendent, which seemed like a match and so we said yes. And by the way I claim the shortest superintendency on record. Six month! No appointments, no decisions and no enemies. It's the way to do it. Get in and get out.

On a January day, sitting looking at the list of churches open, I noticed Asbury First. I saw my name there, but it was crossed out. And then by the grace of God and the saintly work of some colleagues late in April (now this is not quite midnight but it's the ninth inning and it's the fifteenth round in the appointment season) down at Watson Homestead and the bishop comes and says, "We want to have breakfast with you." And I called Jan and said, "Either I'm already about to be fired after six months or they are going to talk about Rochester." And in a moment with the gurgling of the stream at Watson. That sense. You know it. You can't quite reasonably tell it. But you can name it and narrate it. There is something else at work. And the rest is history. Happy in God. The wind blowing at midnight.

Which brings us to April 21st 2005. After many conversations for weeks and a couple of months with Boston University we had heard nothing directly. Email and voice mail were to no avail to have the detail needed. So we figured that the opportunity was going another way and they had made another choice and in the meantime we had a conversation about an alternative possibility available. We considered that other possibility for leadership, and after some struggle gave a tentative decision and gave a provisional "yes" and said we would go in another direction. You know how you are when you are getting ready for a week of meetings. Jan and I decided to go to Kingston for a couple of nights and before we went we readied the house and I went and had my suit pressed and went to the barber. You need to have a barber who has a philosophy and a world view hopefully different from you own. I got the haircut, got the shoes shined, went to the office and got the last voice mail. Ready to go, I pulled into the driveway, Jan got into the car and she said, "Bob I almost didn't do this but I just took the messages off the phone at home and it's Boston University and they really want you to call." And I said and I quote myself exactly, "I'm not calling. I've been in touch with them. They've been in touch with me. It's too late. I'm not calling." Well she had the wisdom to say, "all right, all right." In the car she got, off we drove. Jan is the most energetic person I can name, with one exception, when we are driving. She fell asleep. And something happened in that sunlit afternoon and I made a phone call. And it wasn't what I expected. It wasn't that usual courtesy call at the end of a deliberation. The world opened. And you know what is a match and you know what is a match made in heaven and you know what is a marriage and you know what is a marriage made in heaven. We made a literal u-turn in life and ministry and travel and headed to Boston with no good clothes. I wonder how to think about that. What would have happened if Jan had not taken the messages? What would have happened if she hadn't had the wisdom to let me stew in my own irritation? What would have happened if she hadn't fallen asleep?

How do you explain that? No. The wind can blow at midnight and it's not finally reducible to the reason. Which is why this gospel today and all this narrative is meant heavily to address your soul with this question.

Have you pondered an encounter with the mighty gale of God that can come at the last hour? That requires of us something. It requires of us faith to make a choice in a decision with Ruth and Rachel and Sara. It requires of us faith to trust even when that trust means a new path. Our friend in Boston said, "Bob, I'm trying to make this the hardest decision of your life." And it was. Not for the reasons he thought, but because we knew there would be disappointment internal and external, near and far. Through this hard wind late at night, in our own experience, we learned something about the presence and grace of God.

CONCLUSION

The wind of God blows. Sometimes you hear the sound of it and you do not whence it come or withers it goes. It comes sometimes right at the end. Which is why, in the end, we will close with a verse from Robert Frost. We have been counseled to name and narrate such experience with scripture and Paul of Tarsus, with tradition and Rosa Parks, with reason and John Wesley and with experience of our own. Your experience counts.

The gospel today asks you: can you name and narrate the wind at midnight?

21

Elmira

The Saving Power of an Intervening Word

1 Samuel 25:32–37

You probably don't remember me. I have been here many times, sitting in the balcony or in a back pew. I don't stay around to drink coffee or chat. I feel welcome, but, well, it is just too hard. I'm glad you welcome me though, and I do appreciate the thought. If I can just get free some day and be on my own, why, you'll see me here. I love your beautiful church and the music and the prayers. It means so much to me to be here in front of God. I'm praying God will help me.

My husband is a drunk. Oh, I know that would surprise you, those of you who know him. He doesn't seem the type. How happy my mother was when I married him! "Abigail," she said, "you will be so happy!" Nabal is his name, and he is a successful farmer. Right now we have 3000 sheep and a thousand goats. We live, you know, south of here, up in the hill country, out past the lakes, out near Elmira. Way up south. We live in Carmel. We're pretty much alone out there. The Dead Sea is about a mile to the east, and wilder hill country is just west. We never get down to Jerusalem, not even on feast days. Nabal has his own feasts. He is a devil of a worker. He works sun-up to sundown, sometimes well into the night if the moon is right. He is rough with the animals. Sometimes he is cruel. But he is successful, all right. He could get blood from a turnip.

He works me pretty hard too.

I don't mind the work, though. I mind his drinking. Every full moon and every half moon he gets the urge and drinks. One day, two days, four days: then he is sick and then he is violent. It is getting worse. I would leave him, but I don't know where to go or what to do. What would become of a woman like me alone in the hills of Ein Gedi, far to the south of Rochester? Who would care whether Abigail lives or dies? No, better to stick it out and hope that God will answer my prayer and free me from Nabal. That is my prayer when I come to church. Free me from Nabal. Sometimes I even wish he were dead. But my husband, Nabal, whose name means fool, the drunk, just goes on and on. At least he did—until last night.

This summer and fall he has been mean—almost out of control. He drinks more. I clean up for him. He drinks and gets rough with the animals and with me. Last week he slapped me so hard I passed out. I woke up and he had vomited all over the yard. Anyway, this summer and fall he has been the worst I have ever seen. He doesn't even go out to shepherd the animals now. He sits and lets them roam free all over the hill country. One could get into a cave and die—he wouldn't care. One could break a leg or be eaten by wolves or get lost—he wouldn't bat an eye. He wasn't always this way. I remember when we started out how happy he was, and kind. He would look at his own father, a drunk too, and feel sorry for him and swear that he would never become like that. Never. This summer the sheep and goats have roamed wild, while he has been drinking.

Thank goodness for David, son of Jesse, the Bethlehemite. This summer David has been up with us, near Carmel, hiding in the caves of the hill country. Saul the King has been out to kill him—I don't know why. He doesn't know why. It must be some kind of jealousy though. I told David that if he would keep living the kind of life he has, and especially seek the Lord's will in all things, then he would be blessed as King of Israel and he would be remembered for all time. I told him that no calamity would overtake him, that the Lord would make good all his promises to him, and that he would not stumble or see his courage falter.

I think David liked to hear all that.

But thank goodness that he and his outlaw band were in the hills this summer. They watched our sheep and goats, while Nabal snored. They protected them and us from the Kenites and the Amelakites and from wild animals. Then at feast time, David sent his messengers to ask my husband for some meat for the feasts—it was simple and straight and fair.

But Nabal said forget it. He is so churlish, so ill-behaved, so ill-natured. No one can talk to him. No, he said, no meat. He is like that almost all the time now. He said, "Why should I give my food to this outlaw son of Jesse, whom Saul is going to slaughter soon anyway? So what if he spent all summer watching my flocks? That's his problem."

Well David heard that and hit the roof. He and 400 men strapped on their swords to come down to Carmel and carve Nabal to bits.

So I stepped in. You could say that I spoke with the saving power of an intervening word. I spoke to David. That word spared Nabal's life. That word saved David's soul. That word opened the door of my own palatial future. One little courageous word. Today, looking back, I do marvel at the saving power of an intervening word.

Yes, I stepped in. Not really for Nabal's sake, but mainly to save David from the sin of shedding innocent blood. It is a sin to kill another person. Only God gives life. Only God should take life. So I sent ahead the wheat and flour and animals and wine that David asked for and I met him on the road. There he changed his mind. He repented and decided not to kill my foolish husband. And there he fell in love with me. I could tell. I could feel it.

That walk home in the evening was the longest I have ever taken. To leave the presence of David, who I just knew would be king some day, and to go back to my violent, drunken fool of a husband. God I prayed to you that night! When I got home, Nabal was at it again with his friends. They were wrestling and wrecking all the house furniture. I went out to the barn to sleep. I thought and prayed all night. I should not put up with this, I thought. I should not keep cleaning up for him and pretending for him. I should not keep the farm going while he harms himself and all the rest of us with his addiction. He has a disease and needs help, but not the kind of coverup help I have been giving him. I have really been hurting him.

And if any of you think that covering up and cleaning up for alcoholism is a help, you are wrong, you are so wrong! I should have been meeting with other people like myself and learning from them how to help Nabal and how to straighten out my life. But it is so hard to do. It is hard to admit that anything like that has such a grip on you. It is hard to face that kind of problem. I know. I know. But better to do it early than late. Because there is a point after which it is too late for any help.

I woke up and went into the house. There was Nabal lying on the floor in his own sickness. I woke him, but did not clean him up first like I always had done for him. He stared at me and listened while I told him what I had done for him. I told him David's plan to kill him. His eyes got wider and wider. I told him the feast I gave to save him. I told him the word I spoke to David: "the life of my lord shall be bound in the bundle of the living in the care of the Lord your God."[1] When I finished Nabal had some kind of seizure.

I hope if you are like me you will act before it is too late.
I hope if you are like me you will meet your challenge.
I hope if you are like me you will confront your nemesis.
I hope if you are like me you will act before it is too late.

You may face other demons. You are temperate and abstinent people, so you may not know the drunkenness of Nabal. But you may know other spirits.

You may face the specter of indebtedness, like Annanias and Sapphira. Flee debt. It is a lasting prison. Hear the saving power of an intervening word.

You may face the shadow of self gratification, like Saul. It is a fool's gold, a Nabal's gold. Flee it. Hear the saving power of an intervening word.

You may face the dark ghosts of consumption, like Dives. Flee acquisition. Over time things own you, if you do not own them. Hear the saving power of an intervening word.

You may face the dark horsemen of codependency to another's addiction, like Abigail. (A codependent, when dying, sees someone else's life flash before his eyes.) Flee this slavery. Hear the saving power of an intervening word.

As God lives, life can get better, life can be good.
As the Messiah loves, life can get better, life can be good.
As the Spirit liberates, life can get better, life can be good.

You may just hear that today: that is the saving power of an intervening word.

---

1. 1 Samuel 25:29.

22

Auburn

A Grateful Heart

Luke 17:11–19

AUBURN

Our friend arose early one Sunday morning last month to work on his sermon. His wife found him on the couch, as she came down stairs. From the kitchen she called out that the time to go to church was past. He did not hear her. He was dead.

His body was laid out in an old Auburn funeral home. The irrepressible sociability and fellowship of many Methodists, and many of them ministers, in that old funeral home, in a venerable Empire State city, all the talking and talking, could not muffle the stark arrival of the last day.

Too early . . . Unexpected . . . Unfair . . . Terribly sad . . .

The preacher is familiar with the line of death. Few of us go up home right in the midst of writing a sermon, but most sermons are written and given with that sense of portent. Luther said, "I preach as a dying man to dying men." The preacher knows the quaking fear of the matador, looking across the stadium as the bullfight begins. She knows the sudden terror of the private detective, alone in the dark, who comes upon an unknown intruder. The preacher circles backward in the ring, a boxer avoiding a knockout blow. Matador, Private Eye, Boxer—the preacher is struggling for life in the face of death. I remember thinking of Sophie Phillips, a parishioner in midlife, passing her on the aisle in the benediction on Sunday, only to preach her funeral on Friday. It is a strange vocation to speak about God and about 20 minutes every Sunday, never knowing for whom this Sunday will be the last.

One could take some real pride in being laid to rest almost anywhere in the Empire State. Auburn is no exception. Here with the modern reason William Seward heroically opened the future. Here with a postmodern praise of justice, before its time, Harriet Tubman lived the latter half of her life. Here Lester Schaff found a great open space, an emblem of a global goodness, now a Methodist campground, which was given for the future, a village green in life, Casowasco.

Luke's portrait of a grateful heart is so Lukan. Concern for the sick, the foreigner, the ritually unclean, the measure of mercy. He looks back 60 years, through the fog of time, and picks up some slight traces of Jesus material, hardly to be considered fully historical, and places them toward the end of his 10 chapter personal emendations to the gospel, chapters 9–19, and in the heart of his economic advisements, including the dishonest steward and Lazarus and Dives. We might say, Auburn in view, that a grateful heart, emerging from this memory, needs the mind's reason, the will's justice, and especially the soul's imagination. Reason is God given. Will is God driven. But imagination is God's heaven. Actually, when you pull out the training wheels and attach them, you could think of this as a three point sermon on the well springs of gratitude—part reason, part will, part imagination. One part for modern science. You come too. One part for post-modern will to power. You come too. But one better part mystical and open and gracious and bucolic and spirited and free and open and plebian and all village green and 'better than sex cake' and, well, call it for lack of better term . . . love . . .

A Higher Law: William Seward

In the first place, by all rights, William Seward should have been President. He had the experience and pedigree. He had served as governor of this state. He had lead in the creation of the Republican Party. He had been consistent and unequivocal in his witness to the freeing of the slaves. With a careful reason he had written about a higher law, a law transcending the limited, partial and faulty human laws, even of his own young and native land. He developed and tested his powers of reason as a politician and lawyer. Seward was one of the first to use the insanity defense, in his work on behalf of a freed slave. He reasoned that the investment of $7 million in Alaska would benefit the country, and stood by his decision through all the harsh, short term criticism that his decision occasioned. Seward could not countenance indentured servitude, and in March of 1851 took to the floor of the US senate his carefully crafted sentences. Can you hear his voice?

I know that there are laws of various sorts which regulate the conduct of men. There are constitutions and statutes, codes mercantile and codes civil; but when we are legislating for states, especially when we are founding states, all these laws must be brought to the standard of the laws of God, and must be tried by that standard, and must stand or fall by it. This principle was happily explained by one of the most distinguished political philosophers of England in these emphatic words:

There is but one law for all, namely, that law which governs all law; the law of our Creator, the law of humanity, justice, equity, the law of nature and of nations. So far as any laws fortify this primeval law, and give it more precision, more energy, more effect by their declarations, such laws enter into the sanctuary and participate in the sacredness of its character; but the man who quotes as precedents the abuses of tyrants and robbers, pollutes the very fountains of justice, destroys the foundations of all law, and thereby removes the only safeguard against evil men, whether governors or governed; the guard which prevents governors from becoming tyrants, and the governed from becoming rebels.

Come let us reason together, says the Lord. We need the goods that reason brings. Like Tom Sawyer convincing Huck to paint his fence, and to pay for the privilege with a juicy apple, we need the native hue of reason and influence, at all levels, to open our future.

Peter Drucker, who died last week, spent a lifetime chronicling and celebrating the reasoned contributions of careful managers. Managers who know that the bottom line is not the only line. Managers who know that employees are a resource not a cost. Managers who know that meeting is not working, "one either meets or works." Managers who know how to lead: "the only things that evolve by themselves in an organization are disorder, friction and malperformance." In other words, reason gives us both the leadership of Lincoln and the management of Seward, and we need both.

At the end, Seward opened the future with the purchase of Alaska, a village green moment.

The Courage to Be: Harriet Tubman

In the second place, our preacher friend has further good company in Auburn's graveyards. Harriet Tubman was buried in March of 1913, right there in the Auburn's Fort Hill Cemetery. She was buried with military honors, even as, after much red tape was cut, she was justly given a military pension. By night, and over a decade, she led 300 slaves to freedom, from 1845 to 1860. In the city of Boston, a new statue of her likeness, called 'Step on Board', is found in the South End. Go over some time to Auburn and take the tour and see the home and learn the history. Take your kids.

Here is an illiterate black woman, born into slavery, alone, untutored. One of many children in her own family, somehow she finds her own way to freedom. By inspiration, with the leading call to justice, she returns again and again, crossing the Mason Dixon line and risking death. She travels at night, along the back roads of Delaware and Maryland and Pennsylvania. She carries a pistol. She guides her frightened little groups by the light of the North Star. How can we really ever know the feeling of the cold night along a deserted riverbank? How can you and I ever capture the chill in the spine with the barking of a dog whose ears and nose have been alerted? What would ever give us a full taste of crossing, from radical injustice to real justice, from bondage to at least the first measure of liberty?

Catherine Clinton's new, good biography of Tubman will help some. Take and read. Most arresting to this reader was the fact that Tubman's work on justice did not stop with Appomattox. She settled in our neighborhood. She married. She worked in her Methodist church. She spent three decades using her name and notoriety to fund and build a home for poor elderly people, an early nursing home, named for John Brown, that continued to operate into the 1940's. Here is what she came to on her first flight north: "I had reasoned this out in my mind: there was one of two things I had a right to, liberty or death; if I could not have one, I would have the other."

Many in this congregation resonate more with the postmodern spirit of justice than with the modern insight of reason. You are more Tubman people than Seward people. You want to feed the hungry and clothe the naked and free the prisoner. But justice itself depends on a living faith in a just God, and the courage to stand and exist in that faith. Man does not live by bread alone, and the feeding of bread alone will not bring salvation. Seward is good. Tubman is good. The reason is good. The will is good. But the future belongs to neither. The future, our Christian future, lies with the imagination.

At the end, Tubman opened the future with the construction of a nursing home, a village green moment.

A Village Green: Lester Schaff

In the third place, waiting in the funeral parlor to bid farewell to my brother preacher, and to offer his wife condolence, and intermittently irritated by the far too jovial, too ordinary comportment of the throng, I looked south, in the mind's eye, to an open space, part of the one great spiritual village green that is the reign of God, to our retreat center, Casowasco.

Here is a place where our own mothers and daughters have recently experienced the mystical Christ, along a kind of village green. Here is a space where our men, following 9/11, debated and discerned the nature of just war, along a sort of village green, the great outdoors of the Christian tradition. Here is a place where young people meet and fall in love, where younger grow in grace and in the knowledge and love of God, where older allow memory and hope to coalesce, as decade unfolds to decade.

Reason brings some healing to the human condition. William Seward teaches us so. Will brings some healing to the human condition. Harriet Tubman teaches us so. But the Gospel is more than science and justice! Not less than science and justice, but much more! No reasoned advances will make life more human without a human faith in a loving God, personal and powerful. No marches for justice will last, nor prevail, without connection to the one great march to Zion. Our century needs a *grateful heart*, a kindled imagination, to temper reason and to sustain justice, and to open future life onto a spiritual village green.

As an infant I with others crawled along Casowasco's lakeside green. The property and buildings were a gift, a healing gift. Owned by the Case family, whose fortune, like some of those in Rochester, was made in the film industry, the beautiful lawns, hiking trails, spacious lovely buildings, and grand waterfronts were a gift to God and the future, made by the Case family, of Case\Fox, later 20th Century Fox. The Auburn District Superintendent, Dr. Lester Schaff, met with the family and suggested the gift. I would like to think he said the following, though no one knows. But he was a good preacher and a Union graduate:

Friends, in gratitude for what you have been given in life, why not make a gift that opens life for others? Space for children to grow. Space for youth to find faith. Space for young adults to fall in love. Space for singing, for laughter, for prayer. Space for worship and learning and love. You have been given many things. You have been "healed." Now why not stop, prostrate yourself before the Risen Christ, and praise God. Say thank you.

Whatever he said, it worked. It takes heart. I don't about you, but I saw and heard some of that kind of heart right here, at Asbury First, in our own Fellowship Hall, as our new mayor, Robert Duffy, spoke. You could see it, hear it, feel it. But he can't do it alone! He needs the future vibrancy of this great congregation pulling behind him to rebuild Rochester! Of course with you I am also pondering this passage and its meaning for Asbury First. With this we shall conclude.

At the end, Schaff opened the future with the gift of Casowasco, a spiritual village green moment.

WHAT'S THAT YOU SAID?

Albert Schweitzer said once, "Do you love Jesus? Then you must do something for him."

Huston Smith remembers morning prayers with his Methodist missionary parents and household in China, read and spoken in Chinese and English. He today recites the Lord's Prayer as easily in Chinese as in English. After the lesson and the singing, they turned to kneel in front of their chairs, elbows and the seats, and they prayed. They gave thanks. In that missionary circle, on the Chinese mainland, hearts were warmed and formed and made grateful. Here is Smith's simple creed: "We are in good hands and in *grateful recognition* of that fact it behooves us to bear one another's burdens" (repeat).

You have been healed. You are here because you love Jesus. So you must do something for him: turn back and say thank you.

Your heart is ready—the imagination is closest to God. It is your mind and will that take some tugging.

You are in worship, in front of God. Your heart is warming. You know the truth of things, on a day like this. Yours is a grateful heart. You do have a grateful heart. Sometimes you just need an hour or a sermon to remember.

What's that you said? I listen. It is your heart thumping, talking . . .

I want to leave something of myself right here, for others. Like Seward did with Alaska. Like Tubman did with her nursing home. Like Case and others did with Casowasco. His reason, her will, their imagination. I want to leave something of myself right here, right in Rochester, so that another generation of children can be baptized, read the Bible, sing their faith, fall in love, grow up, and learn to love Jesus. I want to leave something of myself right here. I want to give of myself. I want the world to open up a little, with my walking the lawn. I want the future to be a little more gracious, after my time on the green. I want the unforeseen future to have the slight but real influence of my gratitude, right here, right now. I want to be that guy, that tenth guy, the Samaritan, the one who remembered to say thank you and did something about it.

23

Buffalo

By Your Leave

1 Corinthians 1:3; Mark 13:32–35

PREFACE: BUFFALO

ONE HAPPY EXPERIENCE EVERY year at our United Methodist Annual Conference, now held in Buffalo, comes jogging out along Delaware Avenue. If you start at the Adams Mark Hotel and head east, you pass along a glorious promenade: the magnificent City Hall, the Statler Hotel, Chippewa Street, various great homes now in public service, a closed Methodist Church, Asbury, done in by deferred maintenance, beautiful lawns, street fairs, traffic circles, a modern synagogue, light blue high rises. Keep going. You will come to a great cemetery that has awaited your return for years. Jog along down its majestic roadways, its columbarium, its named graves—Urban, Holmes, Johnson—I found it breathtaking in its beauty, especially its central treasure. Down into the heart of the graveyard there is a rounded little lake, pristine and manicured. There is an island in the middle of the lake, supporting a statue of a child. One receives a flickering apperception, standing lakeside, of last things, of leaving, of ultimate concerns. A child surrounded by a lake surrounded by a green surrounded by a park surrounded by a city surrounded by a state surrounded by a country surrounded by continent surrounded by a globe surrounded by a solar system surrounded by a galaxy surrounded by a universe . . . surrounded by the mind of God.

Ultimate concerns, last things, are at the heart of faith, especially in Advent. Paul by sudden announcement, greeting the Corinthians, again identifies their spiritual location, and ours, as those who live by faith following the moment that our Lord has take his leave. Is it not striking that the central act of our religious tradition is forged in the hour of departure, of withdrawal, of leave-taking?

WORD ON WITHDRAWAL

The world around us, the church we serve, the very proximate anticipation of our own mortality, all raise the matter of 'withdrawal.'

One friend said in October, "how you leave something is about the most important thing you do." He was not speaking about congressional debate regarding Iraq. Although, now that you mention it, he might have been. He was not speaking about the time honored rhythms of leaving a pulpit. Although he might have been. He was not speaking about dying a good death. Although he might have been.

How we leave, by your leave, is our Gospel today.

We are promised that "God will strengthen you to the end."

Is there a saving word to speak about leaving?

AN HISTORICAL DEPARTURE

It happens that our country, right now, is enmeshed in a debate about withdrawal, about leaving. If one leaves, it matters how one leaves. Is there any word of hope about our own dilemma of departure?

As a Christian and a pastor I was angry and saddened when we chose in 2003 to invade Iraq, primarily because our action violated inherited Christian just war theory. Now we are stuck in a tragic quagmire. What on earth are we to do?

Could our extrication from Iraq depend on a careful return to and employment of just war principles? I believe it does. Though I publicly and repeatedly opposed the initial invasion (see sermons 12/9/01, 9/29/02, 3/2/03, 6/29/03, 7/6/03, 1/18/04, 7/4/05), I do not see how we can simply leave Iraq in the mess we have created. Here is one alternative, in four parts.

1. Let the USA state clearly that we are not in the business of pre-emptive war, of attacking nations who have not attacked us. Let us foreswear another Iraq. This may give us some internal and external credibility to engage the following steps. President Bush, alone, with real contrition, could do this.

2. Let us return to the United Nations, and use every influence to gather the world community to share in solving a shared problem. Let us advocate an international, multi-lateral military force adequate to the task (about four times the current troop level). Why not name Bill Clinton and George Bush senior to share the UN work?

3. Let us make a national energy conservation policy law, with a one-dollar per gallon gasoline tax, and shed any vestige of thirst for Middle Eastern oil. Our imperial conquest of Iraq can then be turned to self-defense. Assign Joe Biden and John McCain.

4. Let us give the world a deadline, a time line in the sand. We leave by . . . (x). Yes, we broke it. Yes, we failed to fix it alone.

Yes, a new direction gives promise. Now the world community, to whom we have turned, apologized, appealed, and made reparations, must take the lead. The deadline could be a date (2008) or a count (5000 US dead). Ask John Kerry to hold the watch.

Our attack on Iraq violated Christian just war principles. It was pre-emptive, unilateral, imperial, and unforeseeable. In many minds it was thus post-Christian, immoral and wrong. *But these same just war principles could be our salvation, our 'extrication'.* This extrication would then would be responsive, not preemptive; multilateral not unilateral; sacrificial not imperial; and predictable not unforeseeable. Our pacification could be built upon those venerable religious principles that our invasion rejected. The country would be united, the enemy defeated, Iraq stabilized, and the world made safer. For those of faith, such a course would further attest to the promise that God can bring good out of evil, that where sin abounds grace over-abounds, and that liberty and justice still are the 'last best hope' for this small, frightened globe.

A VOCATIONAL WITHDRAWAL

But our spiritual lives are not lived, in the main, on the global scale. We are much more local, in our story of salvation, than that. We are caught up in shovels to buy, gutters to clear, presents to purchase, arguments to finish, investments to make, choices to confront—all in a very personal way.

Paul sees his feisty Corinthians as those waiting for the apocalypse, that is, the revealing of Christ. And though Paul's worldview is not ours (as was said some weeks ago), his world is ours (as was said some weeks ago). We too are waiting for vision, clarity, and revelation.

I remember leaving Hamilton, NY at age 12. We were counseled, standard Methodist advice, not ever to return to town, not to be in touch with our friends, not to linger, but to move, to change, to go on. The new person needed that space, we were told. His family needed space as well. And we would be a long way off. Actually, up route 46, it is about 20 miles, a long jog, but readily joggable in half a day, I now see some 50 years later. The distance was not geographical at all, but spiritual.

Here are some heretical thoughts, after five decades, about vocational withdrawal. They apply, if they apply at all, to the full communion table today, all of us, in all walks and changes of vocational life.

1. You can end a role and not end a relationship. You can. Grumpy superannuated traditional lore to the contrary. In fact, you probably should. Cut-offs, as the family systems people will remind us, are not healthy. Change the role, hold the relationship.

2. In addition, let the relationship live. Your boss is now your partner. Good. Roles have been left behind, but the relationship changes. Let it. Now he can get your coffee. It will do him good.

3. Feel two things at once. You can. You can feel two things at once. You can be happy, honored, proud, excited. And, at the same time, you can be angry, hurt, sad, depressed. Give yourself permission. Your daughter is getting married. You can be happy for her and what's his name. And you can be really sad too that you are such a decrepit, old, has been, so old that your kids are getting married.

4. Ride the wave. You can stand on the beach all you want and holler at the tide to change directions. Try it if you must. Better to paddle and surf. Hang ten. Enjoy the ride.

A GOOD DEATH

Our open table, and the greeting in Holy Scripture, bring us, in closing, to our own personal leaving. By your leave ... Such a gracious formula. But by your leave, your leaving, among nations, in vocations, and especially in your own life, you do something, and something profound. Think about it, and in advance.

David Hempton, *Methodism: Empire of the Spirit*, has recalled for us the high significance accorded by our forebears to 'holy dying.'[1] This spiritual inheritance lies at the root of your commitment, Asbury First, to worshipping well at death. You take death seriously, as you take life seriously. Your ministries of worship and pastoral care at twilight are of the finest order. Why? Because, in the bones, we know that how we die says something final about how we live and who we are. So, in the 19th century, journals were full of accounts of 'a good death'. So, the way one left, left life, mattered to the living. So the full and recurring rhythms of valediction and mourning were at the heart of faith. It was not by accident that John Wesley widely publicized these early accounts of faithful dying. Nor was it by accident that after his long life, his very last hours were recorded in painting, and in poetry and in sermon and especially in memory. His last words, "the best of all is, God is with us." Will yours like his be a good death? Perhaps at the rail this morning we can meditate a bit, by your leave, about leaving.

1. A good death needs a good life. A life of faith: regular worship, weekly study and prayer, active service in love, careful use of time and of money and of trust. Here is what you can do. Worship on Sunday. Lead or at least attend some caring group. Give of yourself in measurable and effective ways.

2. A good death needs a plan. Give it time. Summarize and reckon. See the good. Remember the kindnesses. Do some things: A will. Planned giving. A living will. A funeral folder. A set of conversations intentionally arranged.

3. A good death needs a Savior. Here is the Christ of Calvary and of Easter, whose love has shaped your best experience. Here he is to meet you and speak to you in bread and wine. Here is Jesus Christ, who hallowed the greatest departure in sacrament, and

---

1. David Hempton, *Methodism: Empire of the Spirit* (New Haven: Yale, 2005), 59–60.

stands in the shadow of every great leave taking. By kneeling here today, we place our ultimate trust in Him.

And thou our sister gentle death
Waiting to hush our latest breath
O praise ye
Alleluia
Thou leadest home the child of God
And Christ our lord the way has trod
O Praise Ye
O Praise Ye
Alleluia
Alleluia
Alleluia

24

Rochester

Colorama

Luke 2:1–14

THE CHRISTMAS VISION

Behold the Christmas vision, a realistic vision, a realistic vision incarnate in Jesus Christ!

This vision is meant to adorn every day of your life, like a great and beautiful image of what life can be. The Christmas vision is this world's Colorama!

From 1950 to 1990, every harried New York commuter was fed beauty, at Grand Central, through your Colorama, Rochester. Every young woman or man in love at Christmas, racing to Macy's for that one surprise gift, was showered with hope, through your Colorama. Every last overworked Joe on Manhattan at least could look up at the end of the day and see a vision of something really great . . .

There are three children tugging at parental sleeves, hauling their way uptown to FAO Schwartz. There is someone just arrived from South America, and looking, and watching. There is a young woman, bright eyed, waiting under the Colorama, and walking slowly toward her a young man who fingers, feverishly, a small square box, hidden in his pocket.

The age of aviation has deprived us of anything quite like Grand Central Station. The heart of the city that is the heart of the country that is the heart of the globe, a cosmopolitan village green of life, spiritual and material beings coursing their way through time and space.

Its glory is diminished, though its grandeur and centrality remain. You may place yourself for a moment along the wall of the great corridor. Hear the rush of the wind as the doors close and open. Feel the rolling pounding of the trains inside and underneath, going south and north and west. Smell the street, the peanuts, the pretzels, the hot dogs. If you are just young enough and just old enough you can stand there, here, and have an experience of really being alive, which is what faith is all about.

Spencer Tracy, in the old film, was saddled with this question: "What happens to men when they get old? Do they forget what it feels like to be young, in love, eager, excited, afraid, on tip toe? What happens to men when they get old?" But he has the last word in that moment before dinner with, guess who. He remembers, in full. And so do we.

There, on the grand concourse, you can see a child and know that one day, you may have a child.

The Christmas vision, like the Colorama, is meant to adorn every day, to brighten and embolden and illumine every day. It is a vision, in a word, of peace. Peace in the heart, and peace in the world. This is God's gift to you. The peace of the heart that resists every force of fear. The peace of the heart that resists every wave of guilt. The peace of the heart that outlasts every unhealthy claim of the self. This peace frees you from fear and guilt and self. Nor is the prospect of peace meant only for the soul, but also for the world soul. The hope of peace may seem very dim. But like the great image across the great concourse of Grand Central, this vision still stands. A day when the lion and the lamb shall lay down, and the lamb shall be able to sleep. A day when the violence of this age will give way to the victory of the age to come. On earth. On earth as it is in heaven. A day when the children of Moses and of Jesus and of Mohammed and of Buddha and of Krishna and of Confucius will sit down at the table of brotherhood.

We are fed and clothed, in spirit, by a vision of a time and place where weeping will be no more, an open space where people grow to become fully human, where none is God and all know God, where meeting and greeting and loving are the essence of all that is. Yes, this is a dream, and it is a vision. It is the Christmas vision: good news . . . great joy . . . all people . . . a Savior . . . glory to God in the highest, and on earth peace. It is to be the emblematic decoration of every day and every way. It is the land which we are meant, at last, to inhabit. With ears to hear, you could feel it in the anthem last Sunday. Close your eyes and see:

> *Say to them that are of fearful heart*
> *Be strong, fear not, behold your God will come and save you*
> *The wilderness and the solitary place shall be glad*
> *And the desert shall rejoice*
> *For in the wilderness shall waters break out*
> *And the parched ground shall become a pool*
> *And the thirst land springs of water*
> *And the ransomed of the Lord*
> *Shall return with songs and everlasting joy*
> *And sorrow and sighing*
> *Shall flee away*

Ernest Fremont Tittle wrote of this passage, "The New Testament lives in an atmosphere of wonder . . . The Christmas vision has to do with the final reality and power in the world . . . This vision of the love of God can be maintained on the day after Christmas and every day after that."

Behold the Christmas vision, a realistic vision, a realistic vision incarnate in Jesus Christ!

Is there a better city than Rochester in which to preach about vision? You need all the gifts of Empire Spirit in order to lead a life worthy of the calling to which you have been called. You need hope, truth, faith, wisdom, courage, freedom, health, generosity, and grace. But you need vision too. Without vision our little hearts become raisins in the sun. Without vision the people perish. Without a positive, happy, honest, loving and true vision of what life can be like, we end up angry, disappointed, fearful, guilty, and self absorbed. You people of Monroe County are vision people. It is your gift, and so your task. It is your talent, and so your responsibility.

For once we may remember Pope's hopeful vision:

> *All nature is but art, unknown to thee*
> *All chance, direction which thou canst not see*
> *All discord, harmony not understood*
> *All partial evil, universal good.*

We have been from Albany to Buffalo. Now for this last Sunday we are home in Rochester for Christmas. Here our Empire series ends. Have we saved the best for last? You might say so, though I certainly could not comment. Here in Rochester we enjoy wonderful waterways, gracious neighborhoods, fine schools and colleges, the best of living, and the world's greatest cheeseburger. We also have our problems. Here we remember the visionary women and men of the past. Keep Frederik Douglass and his north star as a daily inspiration: *"If there is no struggle, there is no progress. Those who profess to favor freedom, and yet deprecate agitation, are men who want crops without plowing up the ground, rain without thunder and lightening, an ocean without the awful roar of its waters."* Honor the vision that sustained Susan B. Anthony: *"Failure is impossible."* Respect the vision that has put endurance in the spine of Matthew Clark: *"ours is an open church."* Recall Rauschenbusch and his voice for justice. Keep the vision high!

Here is your Colorama: ¾ of the portraits shot by Kodak staff photographers, including our own Norm Kerr . . . *Autumn in Vermont, Taj Mahal, 1000 Islands, Niagara Falls, Bryce Canyon, Surfers at Malibu, the San Diego Zoo . . . We remember thaa picture is worth 1000 words . . . Yes, these vistas evoked a "rebirth of human spirit after WWII" . . . lifestyle, travel, space . . . They "cast a colorful spell over Grand Central Station . . ."* And, fascinating, this, the vision, the image gave people a place to meet! *"After work, meet me at the Colorama!"*

It is as fit an image as can be named of the Christian doctrine of Incarnation. The word became flesh and dwelt among us. God became human that we might become divine. God was in Christ reconciling the world to Godself. Christ is the image of the invisible God. You are made in the image and likeness of God.

Here is the Christmas vision. You are meant to see and be a glorious Colorama, salt and light for the rest of the world. Keep the vision high, present, beautiful!

REALISTIC VISION

Yet any vision of the future that is to last must be realistic. Too much of our reflection at Christmas stops before the story is fully told. Uniquely, we in Rochester are also ready to affirm and illumine an understanding of a realistic vision.

Our too familiar text this morning places what is most earthly, the blood of childbirth, against what is most heavenly, the glorious singing of angels. If we were not so immersed, so familiar with the passage, we might read it again aright. A Christmas vision, realistic and incarnate. Luke has his reasons for assigning the account of the birth in his own way. In the midst of cataclysmic and empire wide change, this Gospel writer essays a careful reminder, to faithful early Christians, and to us: to us a child is given, a vision of good news of great joy, so real that you can smell the stable, hear the oxen, feel the straw, and, blessed are we, in the flesh.

Furthermore, the utter inconvenience of the marriage of heaven and earth does not escape us, in Luke's imaginative utterance. The whole world is in turmoil, as our Iraqi sisters and brothers would attest today, while Joseph goes for enrollment. The family is torn away from home, as our New Orleans sisters and brothers would attest today, as Mary travels with child. The little body of Christ comes forth outside, unattended, and at risk, as our congregation would attest today, while we are laid again in an uncertain manger. Why don't things happen with better timing?

When earth and heaven meet there is blood on the ground. Here at the intersection of time and eternity, where the line segment of the divine touches at a single infinitesimal point the circumference of human existence, in the smoking cradle of Bethlehem, there is blood, the blood of life. Birth foretold, death foreshadowed, new life forecast. A brush with the Holy leaves the same tender bruising and bursting life. When you are deeply disappointed, and yet you live. When a friend betrays you, and yet you live. When someone moves your religious cheese, and yet you live. When the cuts come and you are on the list, and yet you live. When there is that brush with the Holy, and yet you live to tell the story.

Life is hard. Nothing worth having ever came easy. There are severe and serious limits to what we may expect of ourselves and others. You may be one who asks everything of yourself and nothing for yourself. You may see your children growing in your shadow, and in turn they ask everything of themselves and nothing for themselves. That is unrealistic. We are all more human than anything else. Isaiah needed visionaries and realists too. Every church needs both dreamers and doubters. (It's nice to have some doers too). We need the gifts of faith, as the Erie Canal has taught us, because our vision is made real in life. And that takes Spirit. It takes an Empire Spirit of Hope, Truth, Faith, Wisdom, Freedom, Courage, Health, Gratitude, Grace . . . and Vision.

New York City: The View from Ellis Island: "the joyful memory of past deliverance gives the power to withstand current confinement."

Albany: Crossing the Hudson: "Let us cross over the Hudson, from the quiet eastern shore of what is good and partly true, to the capitol city of what is great and really true."

Utica: The Far Side of Fear: "We are delivered from captivity, from the power of fear, in the announcement of the Gospel. It is the word of faith that delivers us from enslavement to fear. From separation anxiety, survival anxiety, performance anxiety, anxiety about anxiety. The good news carries us to the far side of fear."

Ithaca: After the Fall: "Failure is a part of life. Wisdom teaches us to admit it, assess it, and accept it."

Lake Placid: A Survey of Freedom: "The Bible is a book about freedom . . . God is loving us into love and freeing us into freedom."

Syracuse: Wind at Midnight!:

Elmira: The Saving Power of an Intervening Word: "You may just hear that today, the saving power of an intervening word."

Auburn: A Grateful Heart: "I want the unforeseen future to have the slight but real influence of my gratitude, right here and right now."

Buffalo: By Your Leave: "How you leave something is just about the most important thing you do."

Rochester: Colorama: "Where there is no vision, the people perish."

I mean no disparagement of the great 19th century Rochester luminaries when saying that for the future, for a global village green, it is Christopher Lasch, whose trenchant, sober, honest realism brought a needed correction to some of the more wooly thinking of the last generation. Yes, he shared, before his 1994 death, an abiding vision of a 'true and only heaven.' But he did so with care, and with caution. Every community—every church—needs some equivalent of his realistic vision. Here is some introduction to what Lasch wrote.

> Lasch is at his Arnoldian best when he observes that tolerance for diversity does not require a lowering or selective application of standards . . . "the spiritual discipline against self-righteousness is the very essence of religion." A person with "a proper understanding of religion," he says, would see it not as "a source of intellectual and emotional security," but as "a challenge to complacency and pride." . . . "The latest variation on this familiar theme," he writes, "its reductio ad absurdum, is that a respect for cultural diversity forbids us to impose the standards of privileged groups on the victims of oppression." What this amounts to is "a recipe for

universal incompetence." It is also a prescription for spiritual anemia. Partisans of "cultural diversity" reject the idea that there are "impersonal virtues like fortitude, workmanship, moral courage, honesty, and respect for adversaries." But Lasch is right that if we believe in these things, we must be prepared to recommend them to everyone. "Unless we are prepared to make demands on one another, we can enjoy only the most rudimentary kind of common life." . . . Common standards "are absolutely indispensable to a democratic society," not least because "double standards mean second-class citizenship."

A REALISTIC VISION INCARNATE IN JESUS CHRIST

So now where do vision and realism meet? Where the intersection of heaven and earth, of divine life and human frailty? Where the incarnation?

Here let us pause for a moment with the shepherds. They listen. I love that about them, the wonder and waiting quiet that El Greco paints upon their silent faces. They listen. Do you know people who really listen? Listen . . .

There is Mr. Haxton, whose window adorns the balcony, whispering from another realm, "peace on earth, good will to all . . ."

There is your family, your mom or dad, whose gifts lifted this great roof, whispering from another realm, "peace on earth, good will to all . . ."

There is dear Weldon Crossland, thirty years of building and thirty months to enjoy it, whispering from another realm, "peace on earth, good will to all . . ."

Barbara Ehrenreich wrote recently of the utilitarian mega churches that she has studied: "they constitute a realm drained of all transcendence and beauty." How sad. Your forebears lived otherwise.

The people who gave us this great nave built for others. They did not build for themselves. They built for others. They built for the whole county, all 980,000. They built for the century to come with Indiana limestone to last forever. They were thinking of others when they built this church. Some of your parents built this church so that you could enjoy and enhance it. They were building for others.

Funny, in Methodism we used to do well two things every day before we even had breakfast. We preached with tongues of men and angels, and we built and built and built and built. Churches, schools, hospitals, colleges, seminaries. Sturges Hall at OWU was built in 1855. They didn't have anything in the middle of Ohio in 1855! Except a building to house a small Methodist college for small Methodists. In losing our voice we seem also to have lost our hammer. We preached and built and then had breakfast and the rest of the day.

You are building for others too. Some of us won't be here to see it finally finished. Some will enjoy it for only a short while. Most of those who receive the welcoming grace of a new space are not here yet. They come from across the county, and they come in year 2040. And after all the bongo drums are back on the curbs, and all the horizontal worship spaces have reverted to Walmarts, there will be a place for immanence and transcendence both, a place for the Holy and the healing both, a space for grace and love. The future will have the slight but real influence of your building, your generosity. Life for others, in the spirit of the One whom Bonhoeffer called "a man for others."

Where is the vision of peace, this realistic vision tamed by limits, ever to be found? Where is the incarnate Christ? He is here. We have celebrated his incarnation for ten years together:

1995: "For all its hideous trauma, the holiday time does cause some people to try again . . . Where love is, Christ is . . . Joseph found the courage to dream and to live out a dream . . ."

1996: "Faith is the courage to start over . . . When it gets dark enough, you can see the stars."

1997: "If there is no struggle, there is no progress. Those who profess to favor freedom, and yet deprecate agitation, are men who want crops without plowing up the ground, rain without thunder and lightening, an ocean without the awful roar of its waters . . . Christ is the image of the invisible God . . . To search diligently for your heart's desire means work and loss and failure."

1998: "It is a harrowing prospect to hear that a leader thinks he can be truthful and 'evasive' at once . . . In Jesus Christ God indulges God's love for us, for who we are—not for what we accomplish."

1999: "The mystery of Christmas is wrapped in the swaddling clothes of the mystery of life . . . There is something about the entrance of God into the world that God has made that inspires a change of heart . . ."

2000: "At Christmas we see the imperious radiance of sheer presence . . . Can you accept your own acceptance? Can you connect with your connection?"

2001: "There is a self-correcting spirit of truth, loose in the universe . . . Will somebody light my candle? . . . He is the way, follow him in the land of unlikeness, you will see rare beasts and have unique adventures . . ."

2002: "Think again tonight about what is real—presents or presence? . . . We get our soul from our limits . . ."

2003: "Without a confidence in pardon we would always, for our safety and salvation, always have to be right . . . Christmas gives birth to the daily, very real, possibility that you can live in a new way."

2004: "Boredom is rage spread thin . . . Hell is to love no longer . . .The location of peace is on earth . . . Christmas is the quiet restatement of what is . . . Too late I loved you, O Beauty, ever ancient and ever new."

Across the expansive concourse of this city and county, there is to remain one great and good image, the image of the invisible God, the Christmas vision of peace, realistic and visionary still, incarnate in the person of Jesus Christ, and know, best, in the Body of Christ, for all its humanity, still best place to find, to be found by, God. As Ernest Tittle said of the Christmas vision: "It can be maintained on the condition that we do not neglect the heavenly vision but undertake to live by it. This condition must of course be met. You can no more keep a heavenly vision if you do not live by it than you can keep a friendship if you do not cultivate it."

www.ingramcontent.com/pod-product-compliance
Lightning Source LLC
Chambersburg PA
CBHW051931160426
43198CB00012B/2112